Peking Opera

Xu Chengbei

Translated by Chen Gengtao

CHINA
INTERCONTINENTAL
PRESS

图书在版编目（CIP）数据

中国京剧 / 徐城北著；陈耕涛译 . —北京：
五洲传播出版社，2003.10
ISBN 7-5085-0256-6

Ⅰ . 中 ... Ⅱ . ①徐 ... ②陈 ... Ⅲ . 京剧—基本知识—英文
Ⅳ .J821

中国版本图书馆 CIP 数据核字（2003）第 061459 号

中国京剧

作　　者	徐城北
译　　者	陈耕涛
责任编辑	张　宏
整体设计	海　洋
校　　对	张行军
出版发行	五洲传播出版社 (北京北三环中路31号　邮编：100088)
设计制作	北京锦绣东方图文设计有限公司
承 印 者	北京华联印刷有限公司
版　　次	2003 年 11 月第 1 版
印　　次	2003 年 11 月第 1 次印刷
开　　本	720 × 965 毫米　1/16
印　　张	8.5
字　　数	100 千字
书　　号	ISBN 7-5085-0256-6/J · 258
定　　价	56.00 元

CONTENTS

A scene in *The White Snake* performed by Du Jinfang and Yu Zhenfei. The hero and the heroine loved each other at the first sight. The hero is lending the umbrella to the heroine to express love.

Foreign visitors to Beijing usually first visit the Great Wall, the Forbidden City and the Temple of Heaven, representative sites of historical interest in the city. In the evening, a tourist guide will take foreign visitors to the Chang'an Grand Theater on the Avenue of Enduring Peace. In the foyer are counters selling handicraft articles, Peking Opera masks and Peking Opera-related books, picture albums and audio-video products. Inside the theater, the stage is of a Western style; seats in the middle and rear rows are soft sofas; but in the front rows are exquisite Chinese-style square tables and armchairs. The traditional seats lend the theater a classical flavor. Sitting in your seat, you might take a look at the Chinese fans around you. They all have a relaxed expression and wear ordinary clothes. Many of them are speaking in each other's ears. But as soon as the gong and drum strike up, they all calm down and watch the play intently. As the plot unfolds, they seem to know who should be the next to come onto the stage and when to applaud a particular actor or actress for his or her performance. More surprising, aside from applause, Chinese audiences show their appreciation for the performance of actors and actresses by shouting "hao!" It turns out that this means simply "well-done" or "bravo".

2

Beijing at night.
Photo by Zhao Dechun.

Peking Opera came into existence in a not too distant past, but it is full of mystery for Westerners. Peking Opera rooted in Chinese culture is quite different from Western drama. You would have a different impression from the one you get from the modern Chang'An Grand Theater if you see a Peking Opera performance in the Hunan-Guangdong Guildhall at 3 Hufang Road or in Zhengyici shrine at 220 Xiheyan Street. For foreign tourists, these two old-style theaters are showcases of folkways in old Beijing. Watching a Peking Opera performance in one of these traditional architectures with old-style interior decorations, you seem to be in the midst of a bygone era.

For first-time foreign viewers, Peking Opera is hard to understand. As a matter of fact, even contemporary Chinese feel more or less unfamiliar with Peking Opera. But as long as you are willing to explore for and understand the artistic characteristics and cultural connotations of Peking Opera, you will find that everything about Peking Opera is so interesting. One morning, you might find yourself in deep love with Peking Opera when you hear singing from Peking Opera fans.

Farewell My Concubine, a movie that wins an award at an international film festival. The movie has allowed many foreigners to know about Peking Opera. Photo shows film stars Gong Li (left), Zhang Fengyi (center) and Leslie Cheung (right) playing roles in the film. Photo by courtesy of China Film Archives.

Photo by Wang Miao.

Intriguing Facial Makeup

Seeing a Peking Opera performance for the first time, a foreigner would wonder: why are faces of actors painted red, white, black, yellow or green? Are they masks? But masks are separate from the face. Facial makeups in Peking Opera are different from masks. Intrigued, many foreign tourists would go backstage to see actors and actresses remove stage makeup and costume. Next time, they would go there before a performance starts to see how performers do their makeup. Luciano Pararotti, the great tenor of international fame, once had a Peking Opera actor paint on his face the makeup of Xiang Yu, a valiant ancient warrior portrayed in numerous Peking Opera plays.

The facial makeup is a unique way of portrayal in the traditional Chinese theater. Makeup types number thousands, and different types have different meanings. At an early date, most faces were painted black, red and white. As plays increase in number, opera artists used more colors and lines to paint the faces of characters, to either exaggerate or differentiate, according to Weng Ouhong, a researcher of the classic Chinese theater. They drew inspirations from classical novels, which portray characters as having "a face as red as a red jujube," "a face the color of dark gold," "a ginger-yellow face," "a green face with yellow beard," "a leopard-shaped head with round eyes," "a lion's nose" or "broom-shaped eyebrows."

Color patterns painted on the faces of opera characters are called *lianpu*, or facial makeup. When a character's face needs to be exaggerated, a makeup type is painted. The most common facial makeup types are *jing* and *chou*. *Jing* is an actor with a painted face and *chou* is the role of a clown. For different roles with different makeup types, ways of color application and painting are different. For some makeup types such as one for a hero, color is applied to the face with hand; no paintbrush is used. For most types of warrior, colors mixed with oil are painted on the face, and meticulous attention is paid to shades of coloring, the size of eye sockets and the shape of the eyebrows. For treacherous court officials, the face is painted white, with the eyebrows and eye corners slightly accentuated and a couple of "treachery" lines added.

A facial makeup type points to the personality of a particular character type. A red face indicates uprightness and loyalty, a black face a rough and forthright character, a blue face bravery and pride, a white face treachery and cunning, and a face with a white patch a fawning and base character. To show kinship, father and son can have faces of the same color with similar patterns. To show identity, a face with a dignified pattern belongs to a loyal official or a

loving son, a blue-and-green face to an outlaw hero, a face with kidney-shaped eyes and wooden-club-shaped eyebrows to a monk, a face with sharp eye corners and a small mouth to a court eunuch, and a face with a white patch to a minor character. Facial makeup can also allow actors to expand the scope of acting. If animals are to be portrayed, there is no need to have real horses and cattle on the stage. For example, in the play titled the *Jinshan Temple*, there is an army of shrimps and crabs fighting an evil character. They are played by performers with faces painted with a shrimp or crab. With novel patterns, bright colors, standard or wry contours and thick or thin lines, facial makeup can arouse the interest of the audience and add interest to Peking Opera performances.

Jing characters are also called "painted faces." As the name suggests, they wear faces with complicated patterns, and different *jing* characters have different painted faces. But the clown, or *chou*, in Peking Opera was the earliest character to have a painted face. Compared with *jing* characters, clowns have a simple facial makeup, though it is not limited to a white patch on the face. Clowns usually make a greater impression on the audience than *jing* characters.

After years of development, there have been established rules on how to paint faces and what different facial patterns represent. Types of facial

Third-year students of the China Opera School learn to paint faces. Photo taken in 1964.

makeup reveal the Chinese people's evaluation of historical figures. For example, Cao Cao, a Han Dynasty prime minister, and Yan Song, a Ming Dynasty prime minister, wear a white face, indicating they are treacherous and cunning; Guan Yu, a general of the Three Kingdoms period, has a dignified red face, showing he was a loyal person; and Judge Bao wears a black face, meaning he was impartial and incorruptible as a judge.

Making facial makeup is a special skill for Peking Opera professionals. Zhang Jinliang, a famous clown player, is able to make close to 1,000 varieties of facial makeup. This is a self-portrait of Zhang Jinliang who played Chong Gongdao in *Yu Tang Chun the Courtesan*.

Knowledge of facial makeup can help audiences understand the plot of Peking Opera. While facial makeup develops in operatic performance, masks have not been banished. In propitious and mythological plays, characters use masks called, for example, "god of wealth mask" and "god of thunder mask." In some plays, facial makeup and masks appear on the stage at the same time.

A male clown. Painted by Zhang Jinliang.

A female clown. Painted by Zhang Jinliang.

For foreigners, the facial makeup in Peking Opera is quite mysterious. As a symbol of Peking Opera culture, facial patterns appear on an increasing number of handicraft articles that hold a strong appeal to people. Even in fashion design, the Peking Opera makeup has become a chic factor shown on the T-shaped runway. Together with clothes, it has entered the life of people today.

Portrait of an opera character made by an official painter of the Qing court. The style of the facial makeup is rather old. Photo by courtesy of Beijing Library.

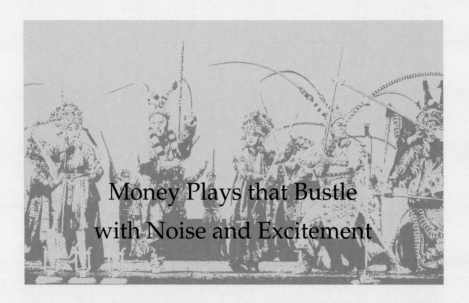

Money Plays that Bustle with Noise and Excitement

Old timers in Beijing liked to visit temple fairs in a bygone era. They were held at different locations in the city during the Spring Festival, or the Chinese New Year, bringing great joy to children and adults alike. Peddlers sold a toy called the Golden Cudgel, a weapon used by the Monkey King, the hero in the classic novel *Pilgrimage to the West*. Children would buy a cudgel home and wield it the way the Monkey King was supposed to do. Of course, children could also tell one or two stories about the Monkey King and mimicked his habitual act of ear tweaking and cheek scratching.

The Monkey King is a popular opera character in China. Every Chinese likes this intelligent, resourceful, daring and just spirit, whose name is Sun Wukong. Children use the Monkey King mask and his golden cudgel to mimic his many feats.

Foreigners interested in Peking Opera are usually invited to see a Monkey King play. They will be dazzled by a group of hyperactive actors jumping and making summersaults like monkeys on the stage. The actor playing the omnipotent Monkey King will invariably leave a deep impression on the audience.

The monkey play in Peking Opera comes from *kunqu* opera, which originated in Suzhou, east China. Today, usually male actors play the role of the Monkey King.

A performer needs to master a whole set of monkey-playing skills, portraying the Monkey King's breadth of vision as well as his resourcefulness, liveliness and adroitness. A few Peking Opera actors made their name by playing the Monkey King. They include Yang Yuelou (1844-1889) and Yang Xiaolou (1878-1938), who were father and son, Li Shaochun (1919-1975), Li Wanchun (1911-1985) and Ye Shenzhang (1912-1966). During 1937-1942, Monkey King plays had their heyday in Beijing. Often the Monkey King was staged in several theaters at the same time. Some theatrical companies even specialized in staging Monkey King plays, offering shows in series. In 1926, Peking Opera actors Yang Xiaolou and Zheng Faxiang staged Monkey King

Portrait of the Monkey King. Painted in the Qing period.

A scene of *Havoc in Haven* (*nao tian gong*).

The Monkey King in a shadow show.

12

plays in Japan. At the time, plays such as *Havoc in Heaven* (*nao tian gong*) and *Water-curtained Cave* (*shui lian dong*), both are episodes of *Pilgrimage to the West* featuring the Monkey King, were popular among foreign audiences.

Sun Wukong, the Monkey King. Photo by Wu Gang.

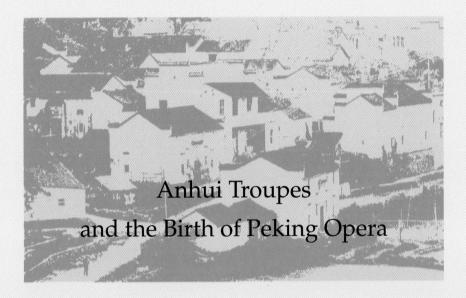

Anhui Troupes and the Birth of Peking Opera

Rulers of the Qing Dynasty (1644-1911) all liked operas. Some of them, such as Empress Dowager Cixi (1835-1908), were connoisseurs of Peking Opera.

At the end of the 18th century, operatic singing in China had developed into several systems. Popular local operas used tunes that included *gaoqiang* (pitched singing), *geyang* (prevalent along the middle and lower reaches of the Yangtze), *bangzi* (prevalent along the Yellow River valley) and *liuzi* (which originated in Shandong). To literati at the time, these operas were far inferior to *kunqu* opera, which is refined and serious. With much disdain, they called these local operas *huabu*.

The popularity of *huabu* had something to do with its popular appeal. *Huabu* plays tell historical stories or folk tales loved by the laboring people. Singing was lucid, lively and intense, and recitations were easy to understand. The ugly ducklings became so popular that many *huabu* companies competed for turf even in Suzhou, Jiangsu Province, the birthplace of *kunqu* opera.

Peking Opera has its origin in *huabu* operas. It was not born in Beijing (Peking). Its predecessor was a *huabu* opera that was prevalent in the middle and lower reaches of the Yangtze performed by Anhui troupes in the mid-17th century.

Anhui troupes had not been limited to staging Anhui *huabu* opera. They also

A village in Wuyuan County, Jiangxi Province, where people can enjoy *Anhui* Opera, the predecessor of Peking Opera.

performed *kunqu* opera, Hubei's *hanxi* opera and the central plain's *bangzi* opera. As a result, these troupes had rich and colorful tunes as well as a wide range of interesting plays. Their actors had developed feats and stunts. Before coming to Beijing, the Auhui *huabu* opera combined the characteristics of tunes of *er huang* and *xi pi*, the former is steady and melancholy, the latter is brisk and lively, *er huang* and *xi pi* constitute the core of the tune of Peking Opera. In addition, the Anhui troupes were good at assimilating the performing characteristics of other operas, such as the recitation of *jingqiang* opera (Peking), the high-pitched arias of *qinqiang* opera (Shaanxi), the tunes and recitation of *hanxi* opera (Hubei), and the bodily movements, ways of portrayal and music of *kunqu* opera (Suzhou). After sixty years of evolution, a unique theatrical variety – Peking Opera – came into being.

15

A three-storied theatrical stage in the Forbidden City in Beijing. Photo by Zhang Zhaoji.

In 1790, an Anhui troupe headed by Gao Langting came to Beijing to participate in performances in celebration of the 80th birthday of Emperor Qianlong. It was soon followed by three other theatrical companies from Anhui – Sixi, Chuntai and Hechun. After doing their job, these Anhui troupes stayed in the capital to offer performances to the local public. By this time, what the Anhui troupes were offering was Peking Opera.

Peking Opera, which had been developed from an assortment of rural shows, had a wide range of audiences. They included not only members of the royal family, officials and scholars, but also merchants, townspeople and handicraftsmen. Peking Opera gradually

became a townspeople-oriented performing art. The Qing Dynasty was in a period of social stability and economic prosperity when the Anhui troupes brought Peking Opera to the capital city. At the turn of the 19-20th centuries when Peking Opera had come to maturity, Beijing had a thriving handicraft industry and commerce; it was home to some 360 guild houses; and service industries catering to the townspeople were also thriving. At the time, the Qianmen area was not only a commercial center but also had a concentration of theaters, teahouses and restaurants; and the Tianqiao and Bell Tower areas swarmed with street performers as well as peddlers and small traders. These not only provided sources of audience for performances in the theaters but also brought new management methods for the theaters and Peking Opera companies.

After 1860, with mobile performances by opera companies, Peking Opera quickly spread all over the country. Tianjin and the surrounding Hebei and Shandong provinces were where Peking Opera gained popularity at an early date. Areas with a fairly early arrival of Peking Opera included Anhui, Hubei and northeast China. In 1867, Peking Opera spread to Shanghai. At the time, a number of well-known Peking Opera actors went south, making Shanghai a Peking Opera center on a par with Beijing. Peking Opera in Shanghai gradually developed some unique characteristics, leading later to the division of "Beijing School" and "Shanghai School." By the beginning of the 20th century, Peking Opera was performed in

Beijing in the early 20th century.

Portraits of Peking Opera characters played by famous actors of late Qing Dynasty, painted by Shen Rongpu, a well-known portraitist active in the late Qing period.

The Forbidden City as seen from the Jingshan Hill in the last years of the Qing Dynasty

Fujian and Guangdong in the south, Zhejiang in the east, Heilongjiang in the north and Yunnan in the southwest. In the 1940s, Peking Opera had impressive development in Sichuan, Shaanxi, Guizhou and Guangxi.

In 1919, Mei Lanfang, a Peking Opera master actor enjoying unrivalled fame then and even today, went to Japan with his theatrical company to stage performances. Peking Opera troupes have since frequently staged performances in foreign countries. And people in the rest of the world regard Peking Opera as the representative of the traditional Chinese theater.

A piece of *yi*. Photo by Yao Tianxin.

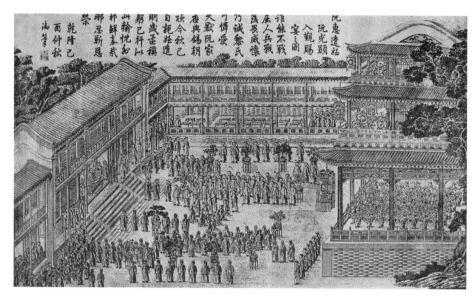

A theatrical performance in Chengde's imperial resort during the reign of Emperor Qian Long (1736-1795). Photo by courtesy of Mei Lanfang Museum.

Today, Peking Opera has become the premier opera type in China having no rival in terms of the number of plays, performing artists, troupes and audiences as well as influence.

In 1905, Ren Jingfeng, manager of the Taifeng Photo Studio in Peking, shot sections of Peking Opera *The Battle of Dingjunshan Mountain*, in which Tan Xinpei played a lead role, using a French-made hand-rolling camera. Photo by courtesy of China Film Archives.

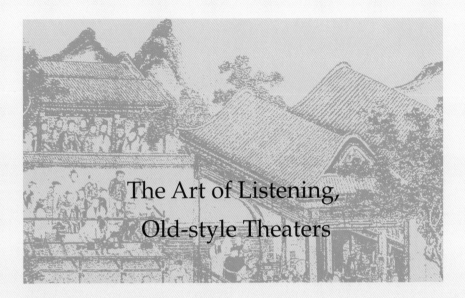

The Art of Listening,
Old-style Theaters

In the past, people visiting Beijing would invariably go to a theater to see a Peking Opera performance. When we see a show today, we say "watch an opera." But old Beijingers say "listen to an opera" instead. What counts in Peking Opera is singing, whereas performance is highly stylized. Audiences are wont to listen to singing with eyes shut and hands beating time. When they like a particular line, they would shout "bravo!" These are typical fans.

Old-style theaters where Peking Opera was performed before the 1950s were called *xiyuanzi*, which literally means "opera courtyard." Facilities in a *xiyuanzi* were rather simple. The stage was square, with three sides extending right into rows of seats for the audience. At an early date in the Qing period (1644-1911), *xiyuanzi* was called "tea courtyard." At the time, audiences paid for the tea but not the opera they watched. For customers, their main purpose in coming to the "tea courtyard" was to drink tea, whereas watching an opera was sort of "incidental." In the Qing period, a show in a *xiyuanzi* could last as long as 10-12 hours, all in the daytime. Customers also paid for snacks such as sunflower seeds and roasted peanuts. Tea charge was not charged until before the start of the last but one item on the day's theatrical program. A striking feature of *xiyuanzi* in old Beijing was "hot towel throw." Waiters, shouting "here comes the towel," would throw steaming

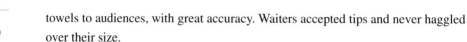
20

towels to audiences, with great accuracy. Waiters accepted tips and never haggled over their size.

"Tea courtyards" were later called *xiyuanzi*, or old-style theater. In the period of the Republic of China (1911-1949), they became known as theaters, and the stage was patterned after stages in the West. *Xiyuanzi*, which was of a traditional architectural style, was smaller than a typical Western theater in capacity, but what audiences heard in a *xiyuanzi* was original singing of actors and actresses, free of a loudspeaker.

In the middle and latter periods of the 19th century, as Peking Opera gained popularity, the number of *xiyuanzi* in Beijing increased, and most of them were located in a flourishing commercial district south of the Qianmen Gate Tower. Viewed from above, the district is situated on the city's north-south axis.

The stage in an old-style theater was not big. Stages were first paved with wooden planks and later covered with carpets. This was to make sure that actors making summersaults would not hurt themselves. At the stage front were usually erected two columns on which were written words in praise of a troupe performing at the time.

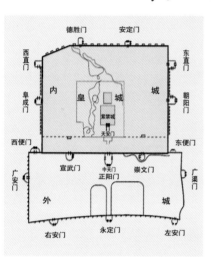

Old Beijing with the Forbidden City at its center. The Outer City in the south is where old-style theaters were concentrated.

In the rear of the stage hung an embroidered curtain, which was the private property of the leading actor of the day. The curtain bore patterns of flowers and birds, in a style compatible with the leading actor. Seeing the curtain, audiences knew who was going to play the lead.

Below the stage was dirt ground. Later, ground was paved with bricks and still later with cement. In an early period, audiences sat on benches facing one another across oblong wooden tables. This sitting posture facilitated chatting and eating snacks but was not suitable for watching a theatrical performance. It is not until after 1914 that long benches with back support were placed parallel to the stage,

21

An old-style theater in Beijing, painted by Sheng Xishan.

enabling audiences to face the stage. On the back of the benches were nailed long-framed planks, on which were placed teacups. At the time, men and women were separated at old-style theaters, with men sitting downstairs and women sitting upstairs. It is not until 1931 that men and women sat together.

At the back of the rows of seats was usually placed an oblong table with the sign "The Suppression Seat" on it. When a play started, fully-armed soldiers came to sit behind the table to deal with any possible commotion. On a holiday the theater owner would hand them envelopes stuffed with money to seek their protection.

During the early stage of *xiyuanzi*, there were no newspapers, nor were there ads and posters. The method of promotion was to place at the *xiyuanzi* gate stage properties for the evening's show. For people who loved Peking Opera, a look at the stage properties was enough for a guess at what the show was for the evening. For example, a block of stone pointed to *The Yanyang Building* (yan yang lou) and

Inside of an old-style theater in Beijing. Women were conspicuously absent among both the performers and the audience, showing that women at the time were not allowed to either perform or watch performances at public places. A man clad in foreign clothes on the second floor on the left does not seem to understand the performance. Picture kept by Wang Shucun.

a big spear *Battling Down-sliding Chariots* (*tiao hua che*). A heap of weapons of different kinds indicated that the evening's last play would be *Havoc in Heaven* (*nao tian gong*). The weapons were used to subdue the Monkey King, hero of the play. A day's program was printed on a piece of yellow paper with a wood block and sold for a penny or two. It is not until after the 1920s that programs were printed with lead types.

Peking Opera had a close relationship with the

A stage curtain, used by Mei Lanfang during the 1920s. photo by courtesy of Mei Lanfang Museum.

Qianmen Gate Tower area in Beijing, which was a cradle of folk culture in the city. In the early years of Peking Opera, the Qianmen Gate Tower area was where the city's entertainment, catering industry, commerce and people's cultural activities were concentrated. It is right in this area that Peking Opera grew and thrived. Not only were Peking Opera's old theaters and the homes of actors and actresses concentrated here, but many Peking Opera fans and people connected with theatrical shows lived in the area, too. In the more than 50 years from the early 20th century to 1957, the Qianmen Gate Tower area was home to some 600 famous artists of Peking Opera, *pingju* opera, acrobatics and *quyi* (folk art forms

The Tianqiao area in Beijing used to be a center of folk culture. The newly built Tianqiao Happiness Teahouse recaptures charms of old-style upscale teahouses in Beijing. Three performances are staged there every day, in the morning, at noon and in the evening. Photo by Zhang Zhaoji.

24

A mural-depicting story of theatrical circles. The photo of the mural was taken during the Republic of China period (1911-1949). Photo by courtesy of Mei Lanfang Museum.

The stage of the Xin Ming Grand Theater in Beijing in 1918. Photo by courtesy of Mei Lanfang Museum.

including ballad singing, story telling, comic dialogues, clapper talks and cross talks). These performing artists had learned their art from different masters and each had his unique skill. At the time, Tianqiao south of the Qianmen Gate Tower was a thriving, densely populated downtown area of Beijing. And Tianqiao's soul was Beijing's traditional folk culture.

The Stage and Props

In an early period, Peking Opera was staged on an interesting stage. The front of the stage extends forward, with three sides facing the audience. The other side is the backstage. An embroidered curtain hangs across the backstage, and on each side of the curtain is a curtained door for performers to enter or exit the stage. Coming onto the stage from the entrance door, an actor with full makeup and costume begins to play his role; at the conclusion of his performance, he goes off the stage through the exit door. This means the end of a show or transition into another part of a play. After 1908, which saw the appearance of modern theaters and the use of setting in Shanghai, people called the old-style stage curtain *shoujiu*.

Shoujiu was made of cloth or satin and embroidered with exquisite patterns. It served as setting but was not limited by operas being performed. It was more like a leading actor's signboard. Every famous actor had his representative *shoujiu*. Mei Lanfang (1894-1961), for example, used a curtain embroidered with plum blossoms, peonies and peacocks; and Ma Lianliang (1901-1966), a well-known actor who usually played old people, had a stage curtain embroidered with a set of Han Dynasty horse-drawn chariots.

On the stage are placed props of a decorative nature, usually a table and two chairs. An imaginary room comes with the presence of a table and two chairs. In the

26

Stage setting. Photo by courtesy of Mei Lanfang Museum.

mind of the audience, the space around the table and chair may be a palace, a study, a court where suspects are tried, or a military commander's tent. Or it can be a boisterous restaurant. The difference lies in details in the decoration of the table and chairs. If it is a palace, the table curtain will have dragon patterns; if it is a study, the table curtain will be of a light blue or light green color and embroidered with several orchids.

A lot of learning goes into how to place the table and chair. If the chair is placed behind the table, it shows a solemn occasion: an emperor holds court, an official officiates, or a general handles military affairs. If the chair is placed in front of the table, it shows an ordinary household's daily life.

There is another interesting point. Chairs on the stage all have cushions, which are of different thickness. Why? In Peking Opera, different characters wear shoes with soles of different thickness. A *sheng* or *jing* character wears thick-soled shoes (as thick as 20cm), whereas *dan* and *chou* characters wear thin-soled ones (1-2 cm). And different characters are required to have different sitting postures. A *dan* character should really sit on the cushion; whereas a *sheng* character should sit on the edge of the chair; and a *chou* (clown) character may move about or even squat on the cushion.

The table can serve as a bed, a support for observing a distant object from a great height, a bridge, a gate tower, a mountain, or even a cloud. The chair can serve as a weapon for characters. In Peking Opera, such a simple method is used to portray a rich plot. When enjoying Peking Opera, it is not necessary to seek realness. Audiences are given great room for imagination. "A table and two chairs" has become a symbolic mark of Peking Opera's "less is more" way of portrayal.

Characters in Peking Opera often ride horses. Audiences will not see a real horse on the stage. Instead, a character holds a riding whip with tassels to show he is on a horse. This is another example of the extensive use of symbols in Peking Opera. There is not a real horse on the stage, but the actor has to portray his riding posture in a distinctive and graceful way. A riding whip gives an actor the greatest freedom for acting. With different pantomimic gestures with the whip, he can show a galloping horse, a horse with a drooping head, a horse that remains at the same place after running for half a day, or a horse that has traveled thousands of miles in a twinkle.

A riding whip is a tangible stage prop. In Peking Opera there are also props of a virtual type. In *Picking up a Jade Bracelet* (*shi yu zhuo*), for example, a girl stitches a cloth shoe sole. While the sole is real and tangible, the needle is imaginary. In the hand of the actress, the absence of a needle is better than an actual

The colors and patterns of table and chair curtains used by famous performers usually agree with stage curtains, or *shou jiu*, they use. Photo shows table and chair curtains used by Mei Lanfang. Photo by courtesy of Mei Lanfang Museum.

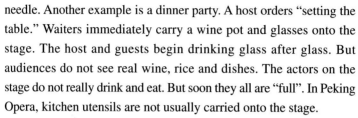
needle. Another example is a dinner party. A host orders "setting the table." Waiters immediately carry a wine pot and glasses onto the stage. The host and guests begin drinking glass after glass. But audiences do not see real wine, rice and dishes. The actors on the stage do not really drink and eat. But soon they all are "full". In Peking Opera, kitchen utensils are not usually carried onto the stage.

Stage props, big and small, as well as simple setting in Peking Opera, including candlesticks, lanterns, oars, letters, paper, ink, writing brushes, ink slabs and pavilions, are not made of genuine materials – they play a symbolic role only. A great variety of weapons as well as flags carried by guards of honor are not real, either, though they bear a similarity to real things.

A Peking Opera is usually divided into several acts. Traditionally, when there is a change of acts, a group of men called stage checkers would change the setting. Wearing long gowns but no facial expression whatsoever, they would come onto the stage after an act is over, reshuffle the table and chairs, indicating a change of place and time, and leave the stage in silence. Sometimes, they would produce some stage effect. In *Inter-linked Military Tents* (*lian ying zai*), for example, to show Liu Bei making his escape in a conflagration, a stage checker standing on the side of the stage would light pieces of paper and throw the burning paper onto the actors, who thereupon do escaping or extinguishing acts – feats worthy of acrobats.

Traditional stage setting is part of Peking Opera's conventions. Many foreign audiences are very curious about Peking Opera's highly stylized performances. In Peking Opera, two pieces of cloth represent a sedan chair; a push and a pull by an actor means opening and closing a window. People watching Peking Opera for the first time may find it difficult to understand. Also, Peking operas are closely connected with the history, customs, culture and social conditions of China. To

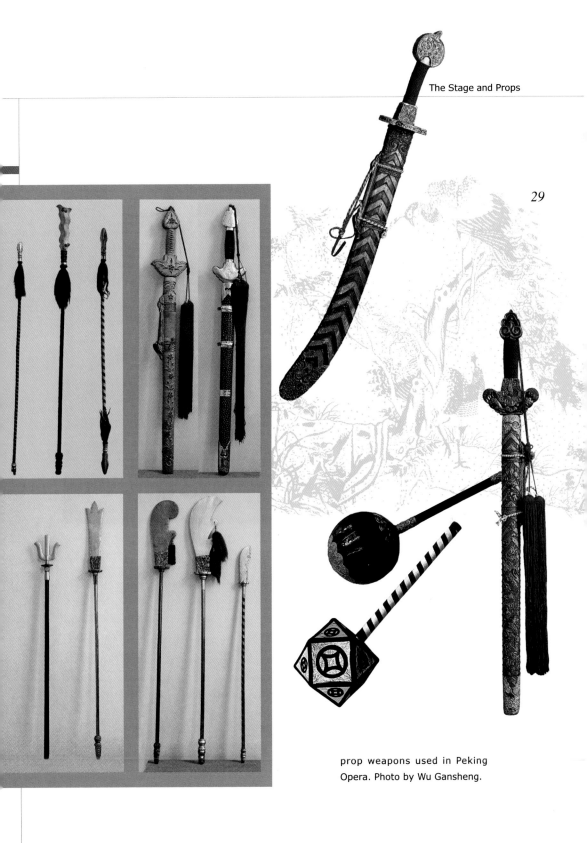

prop weapons used in Peking
Opera. Photo by Wu Gansheng.

In 1927 Mei Lanfang put on a Peking Opera with a full range of real stage setting, an innovation at the time. Photo by courtesy of Mei Lanfang Museum.

enjoy Peking Opera, audiences need to understand China, its history and culture.

Today, a big silk curtain hangs before a Peking Opera stage. A show begins when the curtain rises. This curtain does not come down until the whole show comes to an end. Between acts, a second curtain made of satin rises and closes. This "double-curtain" practice is the result of a reform in the 1950s when the reshuffle of table and chairs on the stage between acts by a group of checkers in full view of the audience was abolished.

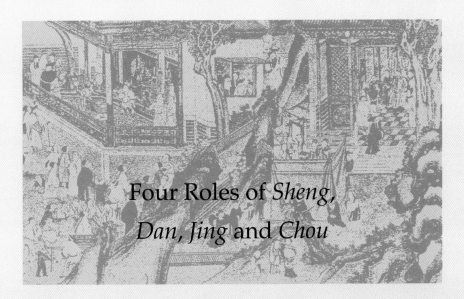

Four Roles of *Sheng,*
Dan, *Jing* and *Chou*

Peking Opera features "character categorization." In accordance with gender and disposition, characters are divided into four basic roles: *sheng* (male character type), *dan* (female character type), *jing* (character type with a painted face), and *chou* (a clown). Each role type comes with its own subdivision.

Sheng is a grown-up male. It can be further divided into four types. First, *lao sheng* playing middle-aged or old men with beard. A *lao sheng* can be of a type specializing in singing, or a type specializing in martial arts. *Lao sheng* is the most common male character in Peking Opera. Cheng Changgeng and Tan Xinpei, regarded as founders of Peking Opera, were both *lao sheng* players. Second, *wu sheng*, or man with martial skills. A *wu sheng* can specialize in long weapons or short weapons. The long-weapon *wu sheng* wears armor, looks dignified and has a moderate skill of singing and recitation, whereas the short-weapon *wu sheng* wears short clothes and is swift of action. Third, *xiao sheng* playing young handsome men, most of whom are scholars. This character is frequently portrayed in love stories. *Xiao sheng* can be further divided into gauze-hat *sheng* (a court official), fan *xiao sheng* (scholar using a fan), pheasant-feather fan *sheng* (a handsome young man), and a poor *sheng* (a scholar failing to become an official). And fourth, *hong sheng* playing characters with a red face such as Guan Yu and Zhao Kuangyin.

32

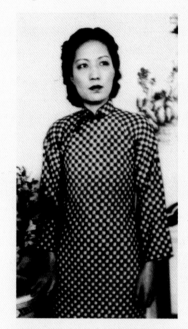

Meng Xiaodong (1907-1977) won great fame as an impersonator of *lao Sheng*, in the 1920s. She played an important role in winning a place for women performers on the Peking Opera stage.

Owing to the uniqueness of Peking Opera, the role of *xiao sheng* had long been relatively unimportant. While many plays give prominence to *lao sheng* and *dan* (female) roles, *xiao sheng* is relatively obscure. In the history of Peking Opera, well-known actors playing the *xiao sheng* role were few in number. Earlier acclaimed *xiao sheng* players were Cheng Jixian (1874-1944), Jiang Miaoxiang (1890-1972) and Jin Zhongren (1886-1950). Later renowned players were Yu Zhenfei (1902-1993) and Ye Shenglan (1914-1978). Among *xiao sheng* impersonators, the only one able to play in shows where *xiao sheng* is the hero was Ye Shenglan.

This is quite different from Western operas where the young hero is very important and is played by highly acclaimed actors. In performance, *xiao sheng*'s most striking feature is singing and recitation with a combination of real and false voices. His falsetto is relatively high-pitched and fine, making the role distinctively different from *lao sheng*. On the other hand, *xiao sheng*'s falsetto is different from that of the *dan* (female) role. It should be strong but not rough. And it should not be as soft and gentle as a woman's voice. Fine-tuning nuances in a *xiao sheng*'s singing is difficult. This is why not many actors have excelled in playing this role like Ye Shenglan.

Dan is a general term for female characters. The gentle and quiet is called *qing yi* and usually represents orthodox yong women. The vivacious is called *hua dan* and represents girls of ordinary households or extroversive disposition. There are also *lao dan* (old female), *wu dan* (female with martial skills) and *cai dan* which used to be played by male actors.

Only "painted face," or *jing*, usually has facial makeup. They are all male with a rough, bold and uninhibited character. They speak loudly, shout at the slightest provocation and, if irritated, may use force. The *jing* roles are divided, too, into the "Singing-oriented" type, or *wen jing*, and the "martial" type, or *wu jing*. Actors impersonating *jing* commonly paint their faces in various styles that range from a single color to bewildering combinations and patterns.

Chou (clown) is the fourth role category in Peking Opera and serves as a foil to the leading character, but it predated other role categories. "No *chou* role, no play" has long been a popular saying. The *chou* role represents far more characters than *sheng, dan* and *jing*. Such characters can be all kinds of people, from emperors, princes and high-ranking officials to peddlers, servants and soldiers, and to scholars, farmers and traders. They can be old and young, male or female. They can be deaf, blind or lame. And they can be kind-hearted, evil, loyal or treacherous. Their humor and jokes are very much liked by the audience. The *chou* role category is divided into *wen chou* (gentle clowns) and *wu chou* (martial clowns).

In the past, when they entered an old-type opera school, kids would first learn basic skills that are

33

Mei Lanfang in *Drunken Beauty*. The master impersonated Yang Yuhuan, a typical *hua shan*. The perfrmance was perfect in both singing and action. Photo by courtesy of Mei Lanfang museum.

necessary for all role categories. Afterward, they would part to pursue different lines, specializing in *sheng*, *dan*, *jing* or *chou* roles. A general practice was that those with regular features play *lao sheng* (old male role), those with a pretty image play *dan* (female) roles, those with a rough voice play painted-face roles and those with a comic appearance play *chou* roles. If it was found later that their appearance, disposition or voice is not suitable for the role they were learning, they could shift to another role category. Actors and actresses worked hard to play their roles well and, after years of performance, their role impersonation would have changed their disposition and even appearance. Observant fans would find that a grown-up male actor with a thin face would likely play a *lao sheng* role and that one with a broad face, a painted-face role.

Two *dan* actress, the servantgirl on the right was impersonated by contemporary *dan* actress Liu Shufang. Photo by Wang Kexin.

At an early stage in the history of Peking Opera, those playing the *lao sheng* role were leading actors. In Peking Opera, *lao sheng* are usually mature male characters with a prominent social status. In the feudal society, Peking Opera once

Ye Shenglan, a top impersonator of *xiao sheng*, or young man, performs with Du Jinfang, a famous *dan* (female role) player. Photo taken in 1955.

A female clown is usually played by a man. This is a female clown drawn by Zhang Jinliang.

played an educational role. Loyal court officials and generals were always regarded as the mainstay of society in all dynastic periods. Their character and moral standard represented mainstream values of the society. In the 1920s, the *dan* role played by Mei Lanfang gained great popularity. Peking Opera then underwent a major shift, from an emphasis on moral education to an emphasis on aesthetic values. Female characters became as important as their male counterparts in Peking Opera.

Two clowns. A white patch on the face is one of the marks of a clown.

A *jing* (painted face) character. Photo by Wang Kexin.

Classic Plays

At an early date, the traditional Chinese theater consisted mainly of singing and dancing. This was true for a long period of time. Plays of this kind reflected people's daily life, without violent conflicts in the plot line. As a result, there was not much acrobatic fighting on the stage. Plays during this period belonged basically to *wen xi*, or gentle shows. The birth of *wu xi*, or shows with much acrobatic fighting, was connected with Peking Opera's settling down in Beijing, the political capital of the country, and with influence from the imperial court. In addition, materials about wars and political events of modern chinese society entered themes of Peking Operas, which led to Wu Xi's popularity.

Wu xi actors assimilated some conventionalized movements from traditional Chinese martial arts and combined them with dancing. These actors are called *wu sheng*, or actors playing male roles with martial skills.

At an early stage, therefore, Peking Opera was divided into two basic varieties, *wen xi* and *wu* xi. This is a classification relating not only to plays but also to performing styles. People called a particular Peking Opera a wen xi or a wu xi. Also, the four basic role types of sheng, dan, jing and chou were divided into either the wen (gentle) type or the wu (martial) type. After the early 1940s, however, the practice of *lao sheng* and *qing yi* being played by leading performers in turn gradually

38

came into vogue. As a result, division of Peking Opera into the *lao sheng* opera and the *qing yi* opera replaced its earlier division into *wen xi* and *wu xi*.

Peking Opera assimilated elements from a host of local operas, including their plays, which are based on historical stories, complicated legal cases, poetic dramas set to music, legends, notes and novels.

Peking Opera re-acts mainly historical stories. But such stories are generally not of a particular period. History here refers to a vague bygone period. A historical story is often a recollection, a pretext for using the past to disparage the present. Peking Opera has a narrow, single moral system that is quite detached from reality but is not entirely absent in real life. Old plays passed down from past dynasties have left behind a formula of "correct" ethical standards for the Chinese people summarized as "loyalty, filial piety, benevolence and righteousness." All these are present in Peking Operas.

Love does not have an important place in Peking Opera. There may be love in a play, but emphasis is on the sharing of hardships by husband and wife or on gratitude instead of on love. Of dozens of popular Peking Operas, each one re-acts a standard morality tale of an uncertain historical period. There are stories about the good eventually vanquishing the evil, and of a lady of noble status loving a poor scholar rather than a young man of her own class and the poor scholar eventually winning an official position. Such morality stories, if deprived of details and certain peculiarities, have a generality and typicality.

In Peking Opera, as emphasis was placed on master-apprentice tutoring, few plays were created and passed on. A Collection of Plays contains two *kunqu* operas and 45 *pihuang* operas that were often performed during the Qing period. Photo shows the cover of the book.

Peking Opera is an art form that centers on acting. Despite the existence of a great repertoire, there are not written plays of a highly literary value in a strict sense. Audiences go to a theater to watch and listen. They do not have to have a full understanding of the plot or appreciate the beauty of the language in advance.

39

Today, audiences usually view Peking Opera through watching what is called *zhezi xi*. What is *zhezi xi*? It refers to one act (*zhezi*) in a multi-act drama. It might not have a beginning or an ending but is the highlight of a drama, which people never get tired of watching. *Zhezi xi*, or one-act operas, are used to test the maturity of young performers and fans. Why? Well-known one-act operas are familiar to the audience, who, after comparing the performances of different actors and actresses in such operas, can tell who are better than others. A new performer must do well in a one-act opera to win approval from old fans; and a new Peking Opera fan must know how to evaluate the acting of a one-act opera to win recognition from old fans.

Qi Rushan, China's most important opera theorist in the 20th century, wrote more than 30 monographs on Peking Opera. He wrote many of the Peking Operas performed by Mei Lanfang.

As a general rule, a successful full-length opera (with both beginning and end) contains one or two acts that can be staged separately as a *zhezi xi*.

A careful analysis would show that the overwhelming majority of Peking Operas are *wu xi*, or shows with acrobatic fighting. There are a great number of *wu xi* operas based on *A History of the Three Kingdoms* alone. This does not seem compatible with the fact that China is not a nation that worships martial qualities. Perhaps this is because the most rapid changes of a person's life occur on the battlefield; or perhaps a person's character and conduct is best seen in a war. Even the failure of characters in a military-theme opera becomes a lesson that strikes a sympathetic chord among audiences, be they officials, businessmen or housewives.

Traditional Peking Operas that have been passed down exceed 1,300 in number. And since the 1950s, close to 100 new operas have been created. Varieties include singing plays, "fighting" plays, plays with equal emphasis on singing and "fighting;" mini-plays, serial plays and *zhezi xi*; ancient-costume plays, contemporary-costume plays, new historical plays and revolutionary modern plays.

Each performing school has a list of representative operas that audiences are familiar with. Many old Peking Opera fans can tell which performer of which school is playing when they see a performance.

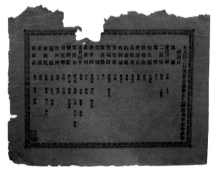

A theatrical program. Kept by Wang Shucun.

The Crossroads (*san cha kou*)

This is a typical *wu xi*, or show with martisl arts. The plot is quite simple: a *wu sheng* (male character with martial skills), to protect a painted face, comes to a village inn. Out of misunderstanding, he has a fight with the innkeeper in the dark. The whole play consists in re-acting the fight in the dark. The stage is brightly lit, but the two characters fight in a way as if they were fighting in pitch darkness.

A table and two chairs are the only stage props. The table serves as table sometimes and as bed at other times. The door of the room is omitted. When it does

not serve a purpose, it does not exist. When the *wu chou* (martial clown) tries to pry open the door, he pantomimes, allowing the audience to feel the door's existence.

With the play emphasizing acting rather than singing or recitation, the language barrier poses less of a problem for its understanding. Watching this play, audiences will see how Peking Opera uses symbolism for character portrayal and plot development. Traveling Peking Opera troupes often put on this play abroad.

Theatrical programs displayed in front of the Zhengyici Theater during the Spring Festival of 2002. Photo by Zhang Zhaoji.

Autumn River (qiu jiang)

This show gives ample play to dancing skills of Peking Opera. It was adapted from a *Sichuan* opera of the same name. But after continual improvement by several

generations of Peking Opera performers, it is now better known than the Sichuan original.

The play has two characters only: a young nun and an old boatman. The nun wants to take the boatman's boat to run after her lover; the old boatman wants to help the nun at heart but feigns ignorance and makes fun of her. The opera, re-acting a boat trip, is full of action and humor. Even fewer stage props are used in the opera than in others. There is only a pole (or an oar) used by the old boatman. Naturally, there is no water on the stage. But simple setting and

A scene of *Autumn River* (*qiu jiang*), in which Tong Zhiling (left) plays a Taoist nun and Wang Sishui a boatman.

vivid acting by the performers creates the impression that a strong wind has whipped up big waves. An interesting example is often told in this connection: the audiences get so used to being tossed about on the river that, once outside the theater on solid ground, they suddenly feel dizzy.

Entering the Palace Twice (er jin gong)

In the eyes of a Westerner, this is a typical opera. There are three characters in the play: a newly widowed concubine of the emperor, a minister and a general, who gather to discuss who is loyal to the court and who should take the reign of government. To a traditionalist, the play lacks dramatic elements. It consists mainly of explanatory singing and recitations. But *Entering the Palace Twice* has not only survived but become an important Peking Opera.

The Crossroads and *Autumn River* are heavy on acting but light on singing and recitation. But in *Entering the Palace Twice* people can really enjoy the beauty of Peking Opera singing. It is commonly known that singing in Peking Opera is not done with a pure Beijing speech but has a distinct Hubei dialect. And this gives a special flavor to Peking Opera.

Entering the Palace Twice has always been popular. No outstanding performers playing the three role types of *lao sheng* (old men with beard), *qing yi* (young female character) and *hua lian* (painted face) do not know how to play parts in this opera. Audiences are only too familiar with the play's plot but nevertheless watch it repeatedly to listen to the singing and compare it with the singing of past generations of actors and actresses.

43

Yu Tang Chun the Courtesan (*yu tang chun*)

This is one of the most popular operas and is also one where every *qing yi* performer gains basic skills. Courtesan Yu Tang Chun, or Su San, is falsely accused of murdering the man she had been cheated into marrying. Old policeman Chong Gong, when escorting a shackled Su San to a distant city for trial, gets to know her true story and recognizes her as his adopted daughter. It turns out that the judge, Wang Jinlong, was the young man she had been acquainted with earlier in the brothel and that the two had pledged eternal love. Wang clears up Su San and the two become husband and wife. Major roles in the play are *qing yi* (young woman), *xiao sheng* (young man) and

A *wu chou* in a traditional play. Photo by Zhao Dechun.

chou (clown). Singing includes all arias of the *xi pi* tune, one of the two major tunes used in Peking Opera. The most popular acts are *Su San Sets out for Trial* and *The Trial*. All great masters were good at performing the opera.

Drunken Beauty (*gui fei zui jiu*)

This one-act play with a lot of singing and dancing is one of the classics played by Mei Lanfang, one of the greatest *dan* players. The story tells of an episode in the love life of Emperor Tang Xuanzong (685-762) and his beloved concubine Yang Yuhuan. The emperor originally invited Lady Yang to a garden to see flowers but has gone to see another concubine. Lady Yang waits for the man who never turns up and drinks wine all by herself. With a heart filled with bitterness and sorrow, she finally goes back to her own quarters. When he plays the lady, Mei Lanfang sought to create beauty in every dancing movement. Yang Yuhuan as played by Mei is beautiful, elegant and poised. Every time he went abroad, Mei would put on this play.

Farewell My Concubine (*ba wang bie ji*)

The story tells the tragedy of Xiang Yu, a great warrior, and his beloved concubine who lived more than 2,000 years ago. The warrior is defeated and surrounded. In the army tent, his concubine tries to lighten him up with dancing and singing before killing herself with a sword. The warrior ends his life with the sword, too. The play ends in deaths but is filled with a heroic spirit. The heroine as played by Mei Lanfang is composed and brave, knowing what she should do in a doomed situation. Her singing is gentle and moving. *Sword Dance* choreographed by Mei Lanfang is the most appealing act of this play.

Lady Mu Guiying Takes Command (*mu gui ying gua shuai*)

The story portrays the great patriotism of an elderly lady. When her country is being invaded by an enemy force, Mu Guiying, widow of a family of generals, leads her sons at the head of an army in battling the invaders despite her old age. This is the last play designed and choreographed by Mei Lanfang. Its premiere was in

1959. The woman general as played by Mei in his sixties is dignified, valiant and heroic in bearing. The play has become one of the classics of the Mei school of performers.

The Embroidered Pouch (suo lin nang)

The play tells the story of how a kind-hearted lady of a rich family is repaid at a time of adversity for the generous assistance she had earlier provided unintentionally. This is a representative play by Cheng Yanqiu in his middle age, which has remained quite popular among audiences since the 1980s. Cheng gives full play to his singing skills when he impersonates the lady.

A scene of *Lady Mu Guiying Takes Command*. Mei Lanfang created the play and played the heroine when he was advanced in age. Photo by Zhang Zhaoji.

45

Judge Bao and the Case of Qin Xianglian

(*qin xiang lian*)

Also known as *Case of an Ungrateful Husband's Execution*, the play is one of the most popular stage performances in the country. It tells the story of a man who forsakes his wife after becoming a high-ranking official. Zhang Junqiu plays

the wronged wife, Ma Lianliang (1901-1966) the ungrateful husband and Qiu Shengrong Judge Bao. The play was made into a movie in 1963.

The Princess Goes to the Northwest to Marry

(*zhao jun chu sai*)

This is one of the representative plays of

Americans put on *Judge Bao and the Case of Qin Xianglian*, a traditional Peking Opera. photo kept by phtotcom

Shang Xiaoyun and his students. The play tells the story of a princess marrying the king of the Huns, an ethnic minority people, more than 1,000 years ago for the safety of her country. The play, which is short and has equal emphasis on dancing and singing, portrays how she departs from her homeland and what she sees along the way through singing. Shang Xiaoyun and his school are good at performing the play.

Hong Niang the Maidservant (*hong niang*)

The play is based on *Story of the West Chamber*, a classic play. The heroine of the play is not the lady but her maidservant who serves as a go-between for the lady and her lover. The maid is clever, lively and warm and has a strong sense of justice. The play is one of the representative works of Xun Huisheng, who was good at playing young ladies.

The White Snake (*bai she zhuan*)

This is based on an ancient legend. *Kunqu* opera had long had this play. In the

story, a white snake becomes a young woman and marries Xu Xian, a young pharmacist in Hangzhou. A monk is determined to destroy the white snake and her marriage. The white snake goes through all kinds of hardship to safeguard her happiness but ends up being locked up in the dungeon of a pagoda. There is acrobatic fighting on a grand scale as well as graceful dancing and melodious singing in the play.

A scene of *The White Snake*, in which Du Jinfang plays the White Snake and Yu Zhenfei the young man.

Borrowing the East Wind (jie dong feng)

The play tells the story of Zhuge Liang, a great military strategist of the Three Kingdoms period, using an accurately forecasted wind to defeat the enemy with fire. This is one of the representative works of Ma

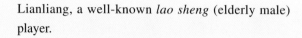
Lianliang, a well-known *lao sheng* (elderly male) player.

The Empty City Ruse (*kong cheng ji*)

This play, like *Borrowing the East Wind*, has Zhuge Liang of the Three Kingdoms period as hero. With an enemy army at the city gate and no army of his own to defend it, Zhuge Liang effects the withdrawal of enemy troops with a show of non-existent troops in ambush, a ploy based on great composure of mind and manners on his part. This is a *lao sheng* play in the repertoire of the Tan Xinpei School.

When Minister Xu Ce Hears News of a Battlefield Victory (*xu ce pao cheng*)

The play portrays the happy excitement of an old court minister upon hearing glad tidings about a military battle. The plot is simple, with dancing consisting of almost the entire performance. But dancing alone can never bring out the character's disposition and happy agitation. This is a representative play of Zhou Xinfang, a great *lao sheng* player. He gives full play to his acting and singing skills when he impersonates the elderly minister.

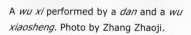
A *wu xi* performed by a *dan* and a *wu xiaosheng*. Photo by Zhang Zhaoji.

Judge Bao and His Sister-in-law (*chi sang zhen*)

In the story, Judge Bao executes his nephew, a criminal. The judge's sister-in-law comes to Chi Sang Town to accuse him. The judge succeeds in pacifying her anger with his justifications. This is a show of the Qiu Shengrong School. Qiu was the most influential *jing* (painted face) actor in the 20th century. He invented a resonant singing style for the painted face in Peking Opera and was particularly good at playing Judge Bao.

The Wild Boar Forest (*ye zhu lin*)

The play is based on *The Water Margin*, a classic novel about a peasant rebellion. It tells the story of Monk Lu Zhishen saving Lin Chong, a wronged general, in the Wild Boar Forest. This is a play featuring the roles of *jing* and *wu sheng* (man with martial arts). When it was staged in the 1950s, Yuan Shihai, a great painted face actor, played the monk and Li Shaochun, a great *wu sheng* actor, played Lin Chong. Their show was made into a movie.

Havoc in Heaven (*nao tian gong*)

Based on *Pilgrimage to the West*, this is the monkey play known to many audiences at home and abroad. It is also a traditional *wu sheng* play. It tells the story of the Monkey King challenging the autocratic and corrupt rule of the Jade Emperor, ruler of the universe. A resourceful, upright hero, the Monkey King represents the weak daring to challenge the strong. Yang Xiaolu was the first actor to successfully play the role. He was followed by Li Wanchun and Li Shaochun.

49

Pi, everyday dress for woman.
Photo by Yao Tianxin.

A scene of *Havoc in Heaven*.
Photo taken in 1961.

Three famous *sheng* performers, Ye Shaolan (center), Tan Yuanshou (left) and Ma Changli (right), put on *The Battle of Wits*.

The Battle of Wits (qun ying hui)

Based on the classic novel, *A History of Three Kingdoms*, the play tells of how two weaker military groups, Sun and Liu, defeat the stronger military group of Cao, by uniting their armies and resources. Characters in the play engage in a contention of wits for the interests of their own groups. This is a play where the roles of *sheng* (male character), *jing* (painted face) and *chou* (clown) all have a part. In the 1950s, some of the most prominent actors joined hands in performing this play to great popular acclaim. Here is the actor lineup and the characters they play:

Tan Fuying (1906-1977) – Lu Su, a sincere and kindly minister serving Sun Quan;

Cover of a *Chuqu* opera titled *Praying-for-wind Terrace*. It became *The Battle of Wits in Peking* Opera later.

In 1956 Ma Lianliang (right) and Li Yanxiu put on *Yang Silang Visits His Mother in Enemy Camp* to celebrate the founding of Beijing Federation of Peking Opera Workers.

A Peking Opera playwright-cum-director should be able to perform as well as to write and direct. Photo shows Ajia (right) practicing acrobatic fighting in a park.

Ma Lianliang – Zhuge Liang, the resourceful military strategist serving Liu Bei;

Xiao Changhua – Jiang Gan, a treacherous person from Cao Cao military group who has come to the Sun camp to induce capitulation, a clown character; Ye Shenglan – Zhou Yu, the conceited commander-in-chief of the Sun Quan army, a *xiao sheng* (young man) character;

Qiu Shengrong - Cao Cao, the cunning head of his own army, a painted face;

Yuan Shihai – Huang Gai, a veteran general of Sun Quan army, who uses the ruse of inflicting an injury on himself to win the confidence of the enemy, a painted face.

Yang Silang Visits His Mother (si lang tan mu)

This is a classic full-length play lasting more than three hours. In the Song Dynasty, Yang Silang was captured by the State of Liao and became the son-in-law of Liao's king. Years later, a Song army led by Yang Silang's mother, She Taijun, came to a fortified city of the Liao to wage war. Yang Silang, with the help of his wife,

52

went to the enemy camp to see his mother. This is a play in which the *sheng* role and the *dan* role have equal importance. Mei Lanfang repeatedly played the role of the wife, while Li Shaochun, Zhou Xinfang and Ma Lianliang, all famous *sheng* impersonators, took turns playing the son on the same stage with Mei.

The first act of the play, in which Yang Silang and his wife of 15 years had a serious dialogue, is often staged separately as a *zhezi xi*. And the dialogue is conducted in beautiful singing. Many audiences are so familiar with the singing that they can accompany the singer in silence.

Grand Wedding in the Enemy Camp
(long feng cheng xiang)

Based on *A History of Three Kingdoms*, the play tells the story of how Liu Bei goes to the enemy territory to marry his counterpart's sister, thwarting a plot to ensnare him.

This is also a famous full-length play with a full range of roles; and many of its acts can be performed separately. In the past, no actor or actress of fame cannot play a role in the opera.

Despite there being a full range of roles in the play, leading roles are *sheng* and *dan*. When Mei Lanfang and Ma Lianliang made a joint appearance on the stage, Mei's name was placed before Ma's. If Ma cooperated with other *dan* role players,

A *qing yi* role.
Photo by Zhao Dechun.

Mang robes.
photo by Yao Tianxin.

The beautiful *wu dan*.
Photo by Wang Kexin.

Ma led the cast. The title of the play, meaning "Union of the Dragon and the Phoenix Presages Luck and Prosperity," is particularly auspicious and the story has a happy ending. The play is especially fit for performance during holidays such as the Spring Festival to symbolize luck. People love to watch a play with such symbolic meaning.

Music and the Orchestra

Unlike the opera in the West, music for Peking opera is not created specially by a composer. Singing follows sets of commonly used tunes. Words are written to fit tunes. The music score is recorded with Chinese characters rather than special symbols.

Music in Peking Opera comes mainly in variations of two set tunes: *xi pi* and *er huang*. Words come mostly in five-word or seven-word sentences. *Xi pi* is lively, vigorous and quick and is used to express an excited mood such as happiness, anger or agitation. *Er huang* is gentle, steady and deep and is used to express a subdued mood such as loss in deep thought, sorrow and melancholy. These two tunes have given rise to a dozen or so strains, depending on tempo, sentence length and theatrical requirements.

In addition, Peking Opera has assimilated tunes from other operas. These include the southern *bang zi*, a gentle melody rooted in Henan that is used mostly by *dan* and *xiao sheng* roles; the *si ping* tune used to accompany sentences of any irregular lengths; the high-pitched *gao bo zi* tune that has evolved from *qin qiang* Opera melody and is used to express an excited mood; the gentle *kunqu* melody used to express subtle feelings; and *chui qiang*, a flute-accompanied tune.

A Peking Opera orchestra is divided into two parts. One is called *wen chang*

whose main function is to accompany singing. Playing orchestral music, it is dominated by a stringed instrument called *jinghu* (or Peking Opera fiddle) and is supplemented by plucked instruments such as *yueqin* (moon-shaped mandolin) and *pipa* (four-stringed lute). Its head is the *jinghu* player. Each well-known singing actor usually has his personal *jinghu* player, who does not show up until the actor he serves comes onto the stage.

The other part is called *wu chang* whose mainly function is to accompany acting, recitation, dancing and acrobatic fighting. Playing percussion music, it uses drums, wooden clappers, gongs and cymbals. The drummer heads the *wu chang* team of musicians and is also the conductor of the entire orchestra, although he generally is not as well known as the fiddle player. The *wu chang* team produces music that accompanies scene changes and creates different stage atmospheres.

The moon-shaped mandolin, one of the main music instruments used to accompany singing in Peking Opera.

Peking Opera orchestra composed of chinese and foreign artists.

56

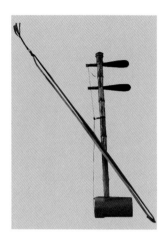

Jinghu, or Peking Opera fiddle with a high sound. This is the most important musical instrument in Peking Opera

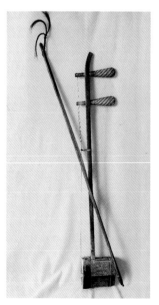

Peking Opera performance is often accompanied by "a deafening sound of gongs and cymbals." People unfamiliar with Peking Opera think it too noisy. The origin of loud music can be traced to a time when theatrical companies used gongs and cymbals to attract audiences for its shows put on makeshift stages, in the midst of the bustle of the markets and streets. But in some Peking Operas, *kunqu* opera music, which is less loud, is used.

An important part of Peking Opera performance is singing, which is closely connected with music. In a theater, audiences focus their interest on performers on the stage, on their color costumes and acting, but the *wen chang* and *wu chang* teams of musicians flanking the stage control the rhythm – key to success or failure of a performance. The orchestra, aside from controlling the rhythm, provides the music itself. In traditional opera theory, a good performance is said to "depend on front stage (acting and singing) by 30 percent and on back stage (music) by 70 percent."

Amateur Peking Opera performers usually learn three principal instruments used by a *wen chang* team of musicians – *jinghu* (Peking Opera fiddle), *erhu* (two-stringed Chinese fiddle) and *yueqin* (moon-shaped mandolin). If amateurs know how to beat gongs and drums to control rhythm, they are fit to put up formal shows.

Erhu, or two-stringed Chinese fiddle. This instrument was not used in the early years of Peking Opera. Mei Lanfang began using erhu from the 1920s.

Acting

As mentioned above, on each side of a traditional stage is a curtain door for the entrance and exit of performers. An actor, before making his appearance on the stage, waits behind the curtain door. Sometimes, he sings a line behind the door and does not appear on the stage before hearing applause from the audience. Sometimes, before dancing onto the stage, he has begun acting at the sound of music behind the curtain door.

Behind the curtain also stands a man whose job is to raise the curtain to allow an actor to go onto the stage. When an actor is ready to go off the stage, the curtain was raised once again to allow for his exit. Coming to the stage from behind the curtain door, an actor walks along an imagined curve and comes to a stop at center stage and strikes a pose. This is called *liangxiang* in Peking Opera. The striking of a pose would be met with cheers and applause from the audience.

Wang Yinqiu, a male actor of the Cheng Yanqiu Performing School who is good at playing *dan*. Photo shows him playing Empress He in *Empress He Accuses the Usurper* (*he hou ma dian*). Photo taken in 1959.

In Peking Opera's military-theme plays, audiences often see a scene like this: two men are locked in a fierce battle; the militant drum beat comes to a sudden stop; and the two opponents come to a standstill, too, face to face, eyeball to eyeball, and remain so for a full half minute. The uninitiated would ask: what if one of them "awakens" first and strikes his opponent dead? A legitimate question. But this exactly represents the ingenuity of China's classical art. "Inaction contains greater strength than action" and "More is said in silence than when something is said" are popular sayings in the country. In acting in Peking Opera, "inaction" sometimes indicates greater martial skills and confidence in success.

There is another unique acting style. Two opponents fight on the stage, and one of them is defeated. When the defeated runs off the stage, the victor does not run after him. He stays put and wields whatever weapon he is using. This is the acrobatic element of Peking Opera. It has always been an accepted practice since the birth of Peking Opera. Such performance is meant to demonstrate a character's heroic spirit. Not until his weapon wielding has won applause from the audience does he run after his long-

People relish watching how Peking Opera performers express characters' feelings with facial expressions and body movements. Photo shows a love story. Photo by Wu Gang.

absent enemy. Can he catch up with his enemy? Of course he can because he is a hero. That is the logic of Peking Opera.

The most basic means of acting in Peking Opera are summarized as "singing, recitation, acting and acrobatic fighting."

Singing in Peking Opera, which can hardly be recorded with staves, is fundamentally different from the music system in the West. The vocal music system in the West is divided into tenor, baritone, bass, soprano, mezzo-soprano and alto according to singers' range and singing methods. This division may be decided by the composer as the musical feature of an opera. The role of a young man may be played by a bass, a baritone or a tenor. So may be the role of an elderly person. That is to say, the singing style of a role is determined by the composer and the singer.

The vocal music system in Peking Opera is entirely different. Each role has its own particular singing style, and different roles have widely different singing styles. For example, the role of *lao dan* (elderly woman) mainly uses the real voice, whereas the role of *qing yi* (young woman) uses mainly falsetto.

In Peking Opera, *xiao sheng* (role of young man) is not equivalent to the tenor, nor is the painted face to the bass, nor a *qing yi* to the soprano, nor a *lao dan* (elderly woman) to an alto. A performer can play any role as long as he or she masters the singing style of that particular role. An actress can play the role of a painted face – a male character, whereas a male actor can play a *dan* (female) role.

Mei Lanfang uses long sleeves to portray physical beauty. Photo by courtesy of Mei Lanfang Museum.

There are some 300 opera types in China, and their differences lie in their tunes, rhythms and phonetics. That is to say, different operas have phonetic features of local dialects. Phonetic charms and flavors often represent the "highest state" of the art of Peking Opera; they include singing and recitations by characters in a play, and even music accompaniment and sounds portraying the elements of nature. It can be said that Peking Opera is first of all a singing art. What makes Peking Opera different from other operas is its singing style. In Peking Opera, the division of different schools represents a division of singing styles. Those who know how to appreciate singing in Peking Opera know how to appreciate Peking Opera.

The *hua dan* uses recitation to express what is on her mind. Photo by Wang Kexin.

Of the "Four Great *Dan* Actors," the one who was most particular about singing was Cheng Yanqiu. This has influenced the Cheng School, which pays great attention to the singing or recitation of every Chinese character, winning appreciation from audiences.

In singing, Mei Lanfang, the most important representative of Peking Opera, sought an overall grace. Perhaps this may be what distinguishes the great master from others.

Recitation, or *nian* in Chinese, tells the story, whereas singing is more concerned with expression of emotions. In Peking Opera, great attention is paid to recitation. A common wisdom among performers is that mastering recitation is far more difficult than doing a good job of singing. There are many fine tunes of Peking Opera that actors and actresses sing to win rousing cheers from the audience; but better performers impress people with *sanban* and *yaoban*, plain tunes of slow or flexible tempos. This is also one of Peking Opera's unique charms. It represents the solemnity and refinement of classic Peking Opera art.

A female general wearing a set of hard *kao*, or armor suit with flags. Photo by Zhang Zhaoji.

Actors use acting and acrobatics, or body movements, to portray characters. Because there are not many tangible stage props in Peking Opera, actors need to make full use of body language to "act" vividly a character's mental activities and details of movements. In Peking Opera, there are many stylized combat shows. Actors use bare hands or small weapons to engage in combat, dazzling the audience with quick movements and imitation martial skills.

Characters in Peking Opera speak out

Yu Zhenfei playing a poor *sheng* who is licking chopsticks. Photo by Wang Kexin.

Acrobatic fighting in Peking Opera. Photo shows a scene of *Fire Phoenix* (*huo feng huang*). Photo taken in 1963.

whatever weighs on their mind. They tell it either to people around them or to the audience. In Peking Opera, even weeping has rhythms, which differ with different characters and different situations. It is precisely such exaggerated acting that adds fun and excitement to Peking Opera. There may be only one or two performers on the stage, but their acting can create the impression that it is a crowded stage.

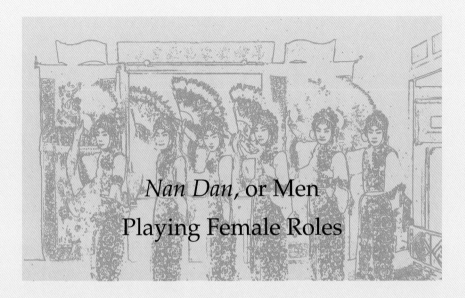

Nan Dan, or Men Playing Female Roles

The heyday of Peking Opera is perhaps when "Four Great *Dan* Actors" reigned the stage. The four actors were Mei Lanfang, Shang Xiaoyun (1899-1976), Cheng Yanqiu (1904-1958) and Xun Huisheng (1900-1968). They were all male actors but played female roles on the stage. With male bodies, they were able to play dozens of female characters vividly. They won unprecedented acclaim when they were active on the stage. Male audiences liked the images of women they played, and female audiences marveled at their ability to play women. Their collective brilliance has shone in the history of Peking Opera, and they have had no match so far.

These renowned impersonators of the female role were born in an era when there were neither female performers nor female audiences. For an opera company composed of male actors only, female characters could be played only by men who looked like women. These actors might

The four great *dan* players: Mei Lanfang, Shang Xiaoyun, Cheng Yanqiu and Xun Huisheng. Photo by courtesy of Mei Lanfang Museum.

Chen Delin (1862-1930) was a grand *dan* actor of early era. Photo shows Chen with his students, including Mei Lanfang. Photo by courtesy of Mei Lanfang Museum.

look like women, but likeness was by no means assured in acting. They needed to learn to act like females. A male actor's body might not be as slender and supple as a woman's, but he can make up for that with postures and movements characteristic of a woman. In the classical Chinese theater, women wear clothes with long sleeves, complying with customs of an era when a woman was not allowed to reveal her hands. When a woman did reveal her hand, a host of finger skills indicated her intentions. With long sleeves and finger skills, a hand on the stage becomes an important means of expression and becomes more beautiful than the natural hand. Male actors were popular also because they were better at stylized running, dancing and acrobatic fighting. Aesthetic requires the quality of being "just right." But Peking Opera goes a bit over the just-right threshold. In a certain sense, this is perhaps because appreciation of the beautiful in Peking Opera has a male tilt.

In the Chinese mainland from the mid-1950s, cultivation of male *dan* impersonators once stopped. This was caused by the query: "What's wrong with men playing male roles and women playing female roles?" As a result, boys who could become good *dan* players lost learning opportunities. It is not until the 1980s that bias against men playing female roles began gradually going away, and there appeared again a social environment in which boys with good natural conditions to become *dan* impersonators had the opportunity to learn Peking Opera. Today, there are many amateur Peking Opera actors who like to play female roles, but because of a lack of training at a young age, few of them are qualified for regular performances.

The biggest miracle comes from the Mei Lanfang clan. Mei Baojiu, Mei Lanfang's youngest son, began learning Peking Opera at the age of 10 and gave performance from the age of 13. The young Mei learned skills from his father and a host of master Peking Opera performers. They include Xiao Changhua (1878-1967, a well-known clown-role player, who served as chief trainer for the famous Xi Lian Cheng Company for 36 years), Jiang Miaoxiang (1890-1972, well known for playing young scholars), and Yu Zhenfei (1902-1993, a master *kunqu* opera actor, able to sing in more than 200 *kunqu* operas, who specialized in playing young scholars in Peking Opera after

In the 1920s the six best-known *dan* impersonators took turns in playing two look-alike ladies in the same play. Photo by courtesy of Mei Lanfang Museum.

A singing performance at Xiao Guang Han Teahouse in Shanghai in the 1910s and 1920s. Picture kept by Wang Shucun.

the age of 30). In singing in particular, Mei Baojiu is generally acknowledged to be the best successor to the Mei Lanfang School of Peking Opera performance. Mei Baojiu has a rich, sweet voice, sings or declaims clearly and accurately and acts in a dignified and poised way. In costumed appearance with full makeup, he is very much like his father, the unrivalled Peking Opera master. His performances in the 1980s reminded people of old - age Mei Lanfang. Later, he worked hard to restore some plays performed by his father in his young and middle age.

In many other Asian countries, it is not rare to find men playing female roles. In the history of Peking Opera, the popularity of male actors playing the *dan* role was connected with strict restrictions on women's scope of activities imposed by the feudal ethical code. In modern times, along with the promotion of equality of men and women and as stage performance by women was subject to increasingly less restrictions and accusation, there has been less barrier to women playing female roles in Peking Opera.

Male *dan* impersonators were once censured by the public. One reason for this is that in the early period of Peking Opera's development, there was a social evil connected with male *dan* impersonators – high officials and noble lords, using their power, forced some male *dan* actors to take part in homosexual activities.

At the end of the 19th century, women began acting in Peking Opera in Shanghai. Female performers then appeared in Tianjin and Wuhan. In 1912, acting by women had also come to Beijing but it was banned in the following year. It is not until 1931 that acting by women and men on the same stage was restored. And "Four Queens," four actresses elected as the best female role players in 1930, posed a challenge to male *dan* impersonators. One of the best actresses in Peking Opera was Yan Huizhu (1919-1966), who learned acting from Mei Lanfang. A famous actress after her was Du Jinfang.

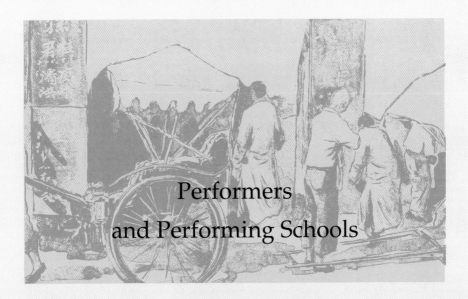

Performers and Performing Schools

Peking Opera performers are a special group of artists. In the past, they did not generally have a high social status. This has changed in the last decades. But famous performers have always been held in high esteem. In their time, master actors Mei Lanfang and Ma Lianliang were so popular that ordinary people deemed it living a lifetime in vain not to have seen them perform.

In Peking Opera, no actor can hope to win fame unless he has devoted years to painstaking practice. Acting in Peking Opera is also an occupation for which talent is important. There are often stories in which the son of a well-known Peking Opera master is but a mediocre actor and is even forced to shift to another occupation.

In Peking Opera, home teaching is recognized, but most people have to enter a Peking Opera school to learn skills collectively before becoming professional performers in a troupe. Cultivation of actors for Peking Opera is quite different from that in a Western-style school. The most striking features of a Peking Opera school are: first, face-to-face tutoring between the master and the apprentice, away from books; and second, teaching students in accordance with their aptitude. In Peking Opera teaching, it is normal for just one or two outstanding trainees to emerge out of a class of students. This method of cultivation corresponded with the need of the Peking Opera market. Peking Opera schools did not intend to produce

Mei Lanfang with his fellow apprentices in a Peking Opera school. Some of them became famous performers later. Photo by courtesy of Mei Lanfang Museum.

stars in batches.

Actors have two important relationships: teacher-student relationship and family relationship. The former involves performing schools, and the latter surnames and relations by marriage. The two relationships are often intertwined. Those born to families of famous actors and actresses have a better chance of becoming famous performers themselves than those born to ordinary families. For an actor, talent and diligence plus a good marriage often ensure a great future.

There are generations of families dedicated to the art of Peking Opera. More than 40 members of the Tan family, of seven generations, have worked as Peking Opera performers. And 18 members of the family of Xiao Changhua, a great clown player, of five generations, have been dedicated to Peking Opera. Usually, family members of the first and second generations pave the way for later generations; the family then has its heyday with a number of its members winning national fame; and this is then followed by a decline. After another one or two generations, the same family would experience a short period of "resurgence."

People often see old actors and actresses playing

young ladies, scholars, pages and maids. Why? People not familiar with Peking Opera would ask. In fact, this is because, in Peking Opera circles, old artists command respect and have the best performing skills. Another reason is that it is a custom in Peking Opera for actors of the same generation to perform in the same play because they understand one another and have better cooperation on the stage. It is only on special occasions such as the Chinese New Year or the staging of shows featuring guest actors that actors of different generations play in the same shows.

In Peking Opera circles, there is a hierarchy of actors and actresses. Backstage, no actor can freely move about except the one playing the clown. Legend has it that Li Longji, a Tang Dynasty emperor who is regarded as the founder of the acting profession, once played the role of a clown. Because the art of Peking Opera is passed down from generation to generation via a master-apprentice relationship, many actors abide by the principle of "once my teacher, always my father." In Peking Opera circles, much emphasis is given to family status and origin. If generations of a family are dedicated to Peking Opera, their offspring will be taken good care of when they become apprentices. It is hard for an outsider to go up the professional ladder even though he sings well. He needs to take a well-known actor as his master at a public ceremony.

In the heyday of Peking Opera, it was relatively easy for actors to make a name. An actor might become famous overnight if he performed in a few new shows

The handsome and gentle *xiao sheng*.
Photo by Zhao Dechun.

69

Tan Fuying inherited the artistic style of his grandfather Tan XinPei. Photo shows Tan playing a role in 1959.

Yang Xiaolou playing a role in a patriotic opera he created in 1934.

in a short period of time and invented some acting skills. But the fame of most of such actors was short-lived. Actors having a lasting fame had enough performing art to bequeath to their successors and have left an indelible imprint in plays they have created or inherited.

There are various performing schools in Peking Opera. Actors and actresses with different performing styles are classified into different schools. For the *dan* role, there are the Mei School represented by Mei Lanfang and Cheng School represented by Cheng Yanqiu. The former is graceful and unrestrained, whereas the latter is deep and distant. For the *sheng* role, there are the Ma School represented by Ma Lianliang and the Lin School represented by Zhou Xinfang (1895-1975). The former is lively and natural, whereas the latter is experienced and worldly-wise. And for the *jing* role, there is the Qiu School represented by Qiu Shengrong (1915-1971). There were once dozens of schools in Peking Opera. The founder of a performing school has unique characteristics in performance, in singing in particular, recognizable to the audience familiar with the actor. In the heyday of Peking Opera, different schools playing the same role type held public contests on performing and singing skills amid support by their respective fans.

Because *lao sheng* (elderly man) actors played the leading role at the earliest stage of Peking Opera, there have been more *lao sheng* performing schools than those for other roles. Well-known *lao sheng*

Mei Lanfang (right) and his son Mei Baojiu playing on the same stage in Shanghai in 1950.

performing schools were headed respectively by Tan Xinpei, Yu Shuyan (1890-1943), Yan Jupeng (1890-1942), Gao Qingkui (1890-1940), Ma Lianliang, Zhou Xinfang (1895-1975), Yang Baoseng (1909-1958) and Xi Xiaobo (1910-1977).

Performing schools for the *dan* (female) role were represented respectively by Mei Lanfang, Shang Xiaoyun, Cheng Yanqiu, Xun Huisheng and Zhang Junqiu.

Ye Shenglan, reputed as the best player of the *xiao sheng* (young man) role, developed a unique performing style after reaching middle age and has founded the most popular *xiao sheng* performing school.

Yang Xiaolou and Gai Jiaotian developed their own *wu sheng* (man with martial arts) performing schools.

After the 1950s, greater emphasis began to be placed on role-playing and the types of opera being played rather than on performing schools. Never have new

Yan Huizhu, a famous player of the *dan*, plays a *lao sheng* in an opera titled *Ceding Xuzhou* (*rang xu zhou*). Playing roles outside a performer's usual range requires versatility. Photo taken in 1954.

schools appeared in Peking Opera circles since then. The audience of today knows little about differences among performing schools. New generations of actors and actresses tend to imitate predecessors rather than innovate. Development of schools in Peking Opera performing art has largely come to an end.

Mei Lanfang and Zhou Xinfang performing on the same stage. Photo taken in 1955.

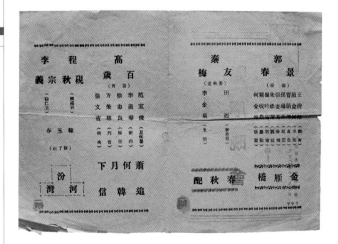

A theatrical program in the early 1950s. After New China was founded in 1949, the government organized demonstrative opera performances to revive the performing art. The program is kept by Wang Shucun.

Women Generals of the Yang Family, a traditional Peking Opera put on by outstanding young performers of China Peking Opera Troupe.

Sisters Tong Zhiling (left) and Tong Baoling, who are both famous *dan* players, perform on the same stage in Shanghai. Photo taken in 1980.

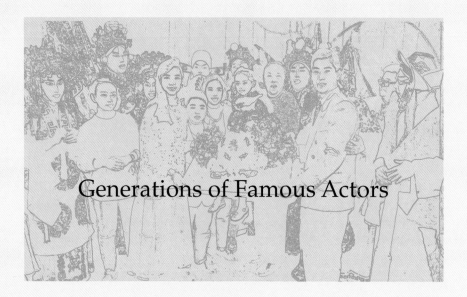

Generations of Famous Actors

Peking Opera has always been proud of the performing art of well-known actors. Famous actors of the first generation were Cheng Changgeng (1811-1880), Yu Sansheng (1802-1866) and Zhang Erkui (1814-1864). They were followed by another trio of male roles: Tan Xinpei (1847-1917), Wang Kuifen (1860-1906) and Sun Juxian (1841-1931).

In the 1920s, leading actors are form female (*dan*) roles. Four great *dan* actors headed by Mei Lanfang dominated the theatrical stage, the other three being Shang Xiaoyun, Cheng Yanqui and Xun Huisheng.

Later, a host of actors playing male bearded roles came to the fore. They include Yu Shuyan (1890-1943), Ma Lianliang, Yan Jupeng, Gao Qingkui (1890-1940), Tan Fuying (1906-1977), Yang Baoseng (1909-1958) and Xi Xiaobo (1910-1977).

Most of the famous actors active on the stage in the heyday of Peking Opera have died.

In its history, Peking Opera has produced masters of a milestone importance. Cheng Changgeng was the representative of the first generation. He is reputed as the founding father of Peking Opera. He devoted the first half of his performing career to Anhui opera, one of the predecessor of Peking Opera; and he devoted his second half to Peking Opera. One of the three most famous Peking Opera actors playing the old male role, he played loyal officials and generals almost exclusively and, when acting, did not allow audiences to applaud lest it detracts from the educational effect of his shows. Cheng sought breadth in his singing to portray the strong personality of characters.

The representative of the second generation was Tan Xinpei, who was the adopted son of Cheng Changgeng. But the two had entirely different artistic styles. Tan sought gentleness and exquisiteness in his singing. In fewer than 30 years after ending his apprenticeship, Tan became unchallenged king of the Peking Opera stage.

The representative of the third generation is Tan Xinpei's adopted son, Yang Xiaolou, who played the role of *wu sheng* (male character of the military type). Before him, no actor had ever achieved what he accomplished. Later generations regarded him as the best *wu sheng* actor ever, lauding him for starting the precedent of "offering beautiful singing in otherwise acrobatic fighting-filled shows." His death caused quite a sensation, with a grand funeral ceremony attended by hordes of people. Many fans thought his death would mark the beginning of Peking Opera's decline.

The representative of the fourth generation was Mei Lanfang. He made his

75

Wang Yaoqing (left), a famous *dan* player, and Tan XinPei in a performance in 1905.

In 1931 Yu Shuyan, Mei Lanfang, Zhang Boju (1898-1982) and Qi Rushan founded Peking National Theater Society. Picture shows Yu Shuyan beating the drum and Mei Lanfang playing the Peking Opera fiddle at the society. Photo by courtesy of Mei Lanfang Museum.

In 1922 Yang Xiaolou and Mei Lanfang put on *Farewell My Concubine*.
Photo by courtesy of Mei Lanfang Museum.

name at an early age and, on his way to fame, received much help from Tan Xinpei and Yang Xiaolou. Mei was an innovator of the Peking school of Peking Opera; and when he sought development in Shanghai, Mei obtained nourishment from the Shanghai school. Mei Lanfang went successively to Japan, the United States and Europe, exporting Peking Opera to the rest of the world.

In the 1950s Peking Opera entered a new flourishing period with a host of new plays created. Well-known actors and actresses active on the stage during the period included Li Shaochun (playing the *sheng* role), Zhang Junqiu, Zhao Yanxia and Guan Sushuang (*dan* role), Ye Shenglan (*xiao sheng* role), and Qiu Shengrong and Yuan Shihai (painted face). Younger artists added luster to the stage at the time. They included *dan* players Du Jinfang, Yan Huizhu, Yun Yanming, Xue Yanqin, Li Yuru, Tong Zhiling, Zhao Rongchen, Li Shiji and Li Huiyang, and *lao sheng* players Li Hezeng, Tan Yuanshou and Ma Changli.

At the sixtieth anniversary of his stage life, Zhang Junqiu put on *Grand Wedding in the Enemy Camp* (*long feng cheng xiang*) together with his family members. photo by Wang Kexin.

Active today on the stage is a new crop of artists, graduates of opera schools. They include Liu Xiurong, Yang Qiuling, Liu Changyu, Li Weikang, Li Guang, Geng Qichang, Yu Kuizhi, Diao Li, Zhang Jianguo, Zhang Huoding, Geng Qiaoyun, Chen Shufang and Li Haiyan.

Ways of enjoying Peking Opera have undergone several stages. The first was the listening stage when audiences went to an old-style theater mainly to chat with one another with their ears catching singing from actors. In the second stage, thanks to endeavors by Tan

78

Zhou Xinfang and Li Yuru in a performance.Photo taken in 1955.

Li Shiji, a famous *dan* player in centemporary.

Shang Xiaoyun practicing martial skill. Photo taken in 1961.

Xinpei, audiences began to see acting. And Mei Lanfang ushered in the third stage when people both watch and hear. We have now come to the final stage when people enjoy Peking Opera via radio, TV, films, and audio and video devices. The theater is no longer the only venue to see Peking Opera.

Cheng Yanqiu (left) and Yu Zhenfei performing on the same stage in the 1930s.

Mei Lanfang, Famous *Dan* Impersonator

Mei Lanfang enjoyed international as well as domestic fame as a Peking Opera actor. The Chinese theater represented by Mei, and the theatrical arts of Konstantin Stanislavski of Russia and Bertolt Brecht of Germany are regarded as the world's three great performing systems. It should be ascribed to him that Peking Opera was known to the rest of the world.

Mei Lanfang, whose ancestral home was in Taizhou, Jiangsu Province, was born into a family of Peking Opera performers in Beijing. He began learning acting at the age of eight, mainly the *dan* (female) role, and at the age of 10 played in *The Marriage of the Fairy Princess* (*tian xian pei*) at Guanghe Theater in Beijing. In 1908, he entered the Xi Lian Cheng Opera Company. In a public poll of Peking Opera actors in 1911 in Beijing, Mei won the third place. In 1913 he staged performances in Shanghai for the first time, appearing in a host of plays including *Romance of the Painted Building* (*cai lou pei*), *Yu Tang Chun the Courtesan* (*yu tang chun*) and *Mu's Village Fortress* (*mu ke zai*). He caused a great sensation in south China. "A good wife should be like Mei Lanfang, and a good son like Zhou Xinfang" was a popular saying circulating in Shanghai at the time, indicating his great popularity. In 1915, Mei rehearsed a host of new plays. After his return to Beijing, Mei staged a modern-costumed new play called *Upheaval in a Sea of*

Evils (*nie hai bo lan*) and rehearsed more new plays, including *Lady Chang E Flies to the Moon* (*chang e ben yue*), *Chun Xiang Upsets the Study* (*chun xiang nao xue*) and *Daiyu Burying Flowers* (*daiyu zang hua*). In 1916, Mei Lanfang went to Shanghai for the third time and performed for 45 consecutive days. In 1918, at the peak of his performing career, he moved to Shanghai, where he staged shows at the Tianchan Theater.

Mei Lanfang absorbed Shanghai's modern drama, new-style stage, lighting, makeup and costume, assimilated the acting styles of different *dan* roles, made innovations in singing, recitation, dancing, music and costuming, and created a graceful, mellow and smooth singing style. He created the Mei School.

Mei had a sweet, resonant voice, which is rare in a male actor. Aside from inheriting traditional tunes, Mei composed a great number of new, unique melodies. Thanks to his innovation, some rarely used traditional arias won great popularity. And he made a point of suiting his singing to different roles and plots. His recitation was rhythmic and clear. The higher the voice was picthed, the sweeter and mellower it became. From his recitations, audiences could hear happiness, anger, worry, sorrow and fright. In acting, aside from using movements from *kunqu* opera, Mei created a host of dances, including satin dance, sword dance, sleeve dance, dusting dance and feather dance. At the same time, he incorporated dancing movements in his acting in some otherwise dance-free plays. As a result, every move he made on the stage was graceful and beautiful.

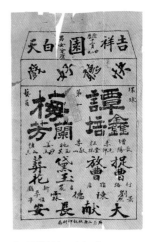

A 1917 theatrical program featuring performances by Tan Xinpei and Mei Lanfang. Photo by courtesy of Mei Lanfang Museum.

82

Mei Lanfang receiving French guests at his residence in Beijing. Photo by courtesy of Mei Lanfang Museum.

When he performed in a play with a lot of acrobatic fighting, fighting was combined with dancing. And generally speaking, there was more dancing than fighting. This is another breakthrough.

In 1919, Mei Lanfang, at the invitation of the Imperial Theater in Tokyo, went to Japan and performed Peking Opera there for a month. Plays he staged there include *The Maiden in Heaven Showering Flowers* (*tian nu san hua*) and *Romance of the Jade Hairpin* (*yu zan ji*).

In 1921, with help from Qi Rushan (1877-1962), a well-known opera expert, Mei wrote and performed a well-known play called *Farewell My Concubine* (*ba wang bie ji*). From 1922, Mei became head of Cheng Hua Opera Company. Borrowing elements from ancient paintings of beauties and statues of female deities, Mei made creative innovations in the facial makeup, headgear and costume of characters. Even in the use of musical instruments, Mei tried bold reforms, too. For example, he used the *erhu* (two-stringed Chinese fiddle with a gentle sound) as a supplement to the *jinghu* (Peking Opera fiddle with a high sound) so as to accompany the singing by the *dan* (female) role. Mei made unique contributions to Peking

Poster advertising a color film in which Mei Lanfang played the lead role. Photo taken in Shanghai in 1949.

Opera in singing, recitation, acting, acrobatic fighting, dancing, facial expression, music, costume and stage art. In 1927, in a public selection of *dan* actors sponsored by a newspaper in Beijing, Mei Lanfang ranked among the "Four Great *Dan* Actors," the other three being Cheng Yanqiu, Shang Xiaoyun and Xun Huisheng. In 1931, after the "September 18" Incident which marked the beginning of Japanese invasion of northeast China, Mei Lanfang promoted patriotism by staging *Resisting Jin Invaders* (*kang jin bing*) and *Life-and-Death Hatred* (*sheng si hen*) in Shanghai. During the Second World War, when Japan occupied part of China, Mei Lanfang grew a beard and

Mei Lanfang playing a *wu sheng*. Photo by courtesy of Mei Lanfang Museum.

Mei Lanfang in *Drunken Beauty* (*gui fei zui jiu*), one of his representative plays. Photo by courtesy of Mei Lanfang Museum.

lived a secluded life, refusing to perform.

In the spring of 1930, Mei Lanfang went to the United States at the head of his theatrical company and put up performances in New York, Chicago, San Francisco and Los Angeles, to resounding successes. During the period, Pomona College and University of Southern California awarded him honorary doctorate degrees in literature. In 1935, he put up shows in Europe with his company and examined foreign theatrical art. Among Peking Opera artists, Mei Lanfang staged the most performances abroad and received the most visiting foreign artists. He displayed Peking Opera art and the modesty and simplicity of Chinese artists to foreigners and won their appreciation.

In 1950 Mei Lanfang moved back to Beijing from Shanghai for permanent settlement. His representative plays are *The Drunken Beauty* (*gui fei zui jiu*), *The Maiden in Heaven Showering Flowers* (*tian nu san hua*), *The Heaven-and-Earth Blade* (*yu zhou feng*) and *The Fisherman's Revenge* (*da yu sha jia*). And he trained more than 100 performers.

Theatrical Companies
and Old-style Opera Schools

Before the 1950s, opera performers belong to one theatrical company or another. Even today, companies of different opera types are active in rural and remotes parts of the country.

A traditional theatrical company usually consisted of members of a clan, who passed on performing skills on the basis of a master-apprentice relationship. A company borrowed elements of other opera types and kept improving performance to suit the taste of audiences in different localities. And it needed to have a rich repertoire so that it would not run out of plays at one location.

A professional theatrical company earned its living by going to places to put up performances. Generally speaking, members of the company lived on a makeshift stage or in tents, and the company paid for its own transportation. Owing to competition between companies as well as natural and human disasters, it was not rare for a company of no particular fame to get into dire financial difficulties. Many performers knew about the hardships of life in a theatrical company and would not let their offspring take the road they had taken. Despite their dissatisfaction with their life, performers, to earn a living, had to do thick makeup, put on colorful costume and played one character after another emotionally on the stage. Such is the life of performers, generation after generation.

A strict hierarchy existed in an old-style theatrical company. A company's manager is called *ban zhu*, or company owner. Opera teachers had the highest artistic status in a company. They served as playwright, music composer and director. Teaching child apprentices the art of performance was their responsibility, and they decided whether to reward or penalize a child apprentice; and they were principal dispensers of physical punishment against child apprentices. Their artistic and skill levels largely determined the artistic level of the theatrical company they served. There was another kind of people in a company called "masters." These were fairly good actors who were free in person and employed by the *ban zhu* through a contract. An apprentice who had learned to play a role at the expiration of his indenture would acquire the status of a "master" and drew a salary in another company that had hired him. Those with the lowest status were child apprentices. Many of them were sold to theatrical companies by their families out of poverty. At the time of sale, their parents would sign an indenture, which stipulates not only the price and time limit but also the term that the death of an apprentice had nothing to do with the company. Once sold, a child apprentice lost his personal freedom, nor were his parents allowed to see him. Kids in a theatrical company began to learn acting and singing before they could read. They learned acting and singing from their performer parents or old performers and learned to read and write at the same time. This cruel system was abolished after the 1950s.

Theatrical companies were divided into two major types: the *wen* (Singing-oriented) company that was good at singing; and the *wu* (acrobatic-fighting-oriented) company that was good at acrobatic fighting. A singing company might hire an actor from an acrobatic fighting company to increase the appeal of its shows to the audience.

In an early date, a theatrical company was composed of artists good at different role categories and different plays. Artistic level of Performers of a company were more or less equal. They supported one another in role playing and their incomes were more or less the same. Later, this system was replaced by a leading actor-chooses-the-cast system. Under the new system, the cast of a play was led by a famous, popular actor, who naturally played the lead. A leading actor had not only an exclusive *jinghu* (Peking Opera fiddle) player and an exclusive drummer serving him but also a person taking care of his stage props. If the actor played the *dan* role, he would have an exclusive "hair doer." Incomes of actors were calculated according to the proportion of acting they did in a particular play. This promoted competition among performers as well as performer movement between theatrical companies.

Many outstanding performers not only played lead roles on the stage but were also bosses of opera companies. They were involved in the creation of every new play, from

A group photo of girl students learning Peking Opera in the Chong Ya Opera School in Beijing. Established in 1916, Chong Ya was the first opera school for girl students. Photo by courtesy of Mei Lanfang Museum.

its writing and direction to music composition and the design of stage art. And playwrights and composers did their best to suit plays to performers who were to play the lead roles so that the latter were able to give play to their performing skills to the fullest extent.

During the time of performance by a theatrical company, there were some backstage rules that show social customs at the time.

1 Women were forbidden to come onto the stage or backstage.

2 The God of Fortune mask must not be put face up; a person holding the mask must not speak to another person.

3 Lifting the curtain for a peep at the audience was forbidden.

4 Gambling was prohibited backstage.

Shang Xiaoyun, one of the four great players of *dan*, founded Rongchun Opera School in 1936 in Beijing. Total enrolment reached 570 people. Photo shows Shang teaching new apprentices.

Ma Lianliang, who was president of the Beijing Opera School in the 1960s, gave a demonstrative lecture to his students. Photo taken in 1962.

5 Sitting on the drummer's seat was forbidden (to prevent unauthorized drum beating).

6 No authorized handling of theatrical swords.

7 No seating on trunks containing props.

8 No making up before the clown-role player has finished doing his makeup (few colors are used for the clown role; this makes painting brushes easier to clean for doing makeup for others).

9 Actor playing female role must not reveal body after finishing his facial makeup. And

10 Abusive language was prohibited.

With Peking Opera becoming more mature, there appeared old-style schools specializing in training Peking Opera performers in the latter half of the 19th century. In the last years of the 19th century and the early years of the 20th century, there appeared a number of old-style Peking Opera schools of considerable sizes. In Beijing, these included the well-known Fu Lian Cheng School (formerly known as Xi Lian Cheng) set up by Ye Chunshan and Qing Yi School set up by Yu Zhenting. Many graduates of the schools went on to become performers of national fame. The next 40 years saw the emergence of other schools, including Rong Chun School set up by Shang Xiaoyun, a well-known *dan* player, Ming Chun School set up by Li Wanchun, a famous *wu sheng* player, and the China Opera School, of which Jiao Juyin and Jin Zhongsun served successively as president. Old-style opera schools of fairly big sizes were also set up in Shanghai, Xi'an and Tianjin.

The music score of *Story of the Jade Hairpin* (*yu zan ji*). Kept by Wang Shucun.

Compared with master-apprentice teaching, learning in an old-style opera school called *keban* was more regularized and specialized. It had full-time teachers and a systematic teaching-learning schedule, allowing kids to receive systematic, solid basic training and have a broader grasp of singing and acting skills. Many of their graduates became outstanding performers. In its 44-year history, the Fu Lian Cheng School trained seven classes of close to 700 students. Every class offered celebrity performers active on the Peking Opera stage for dozens of years. Fu Lian Cheng is the old-style school that had the longest history, was biggest in scale and trained the greatest number of performers

A theatrical program of the Fu Lian Cheng Opera School. Established in 1904, the school trained seven classes of Peking Opera performers until its close in 1948. Kept by Wang Shucun

Newlyweds wearing red wedding garment. Photo by Zhang Zhaoji.

in the history of Peking Opera. In addition, the school preserved, sorted out and created a great number of fine plays, contributing greatly to the development of Peking Opera.

After the founding of New China in 1949, theatrical education received support from the government. The year of 1950 saw the establishment in Beijing of the first national institution for opera education, the Opera Experimental School, which was later renamed China Opera School. Teachers from old-style opera schools taught classes at the school. The school also invited well-known actors, including Mei Lanfang, Shang Xiaoyun, Cheng Yanqiu and Xun Huisheng, to give lectures to students. Since the 1950s, the school has trained close to 5,000 people, who have been active in every field of Peking Opera as a performing art. In 1978 the school was made into China Opera Institute to become the only institution of tertiary education dedicated to opera education in China. In addition, opera schools have been set up in Shanghai, Tianjin, Shanxi, Hebei, Shandong and Jiangsu. These schools also enroll foreign students.

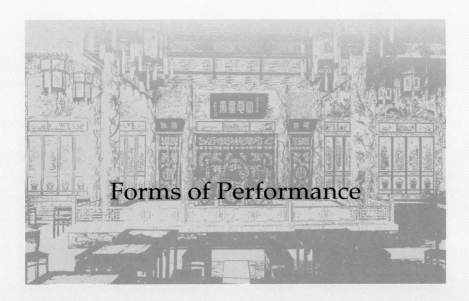

Forms of Performance

Theatre Performance

The earliest commercial performances took place in a teahouse. A spectator paid for admission primarily to drink tea but had to give a tip to a waiter for finding him a seat. Such a teahouse with a stage later evolved into an old-style theater called *xiyuanzi*.

City-based theatrical companies signed a contract with a theater, establishing a system in which the companies put up performances in turn. Performance usually began at noon and continued until dusk. No performance was staged in the evening. The earliest theatrical program was a poster put up before the stage prior to performance.

Many Peking Opera shows were staged in guildhalls that used to line the street south of the Qianmen Gate Tower in Beijing. The more tastefully furnished guildhalls had a stage.

Temple Fairs as Stage

At an even earlier date, Peking Opera and its predecessors chose temple fairs to stage their performances. A fair was a true occasion of pleasure for common Pekingers.

In the last couple of centuries, temple fairs have had ups and downs in Beijing. Of the two biggest fairs in Beijing, one was in east Beijing, at Long Fu Temple, and

The theatrical stage inside the residence of Prince Gong of Qing Dynasty built in 1777. Now, performances are staged almost every evening on the stage. Photo by Zhang Zhaoji.

the other was in west Beijing, at Hu Guo Temple. In the 1950s, the White Dagoba Temple joined the two in offering fair space. Theatrical companies erected tents with cloth curtains at temple fair grounds to put up their shows.

Before Peking Opera entered the old-style theater, theatrical companies made a living at temple fairs. Keeping them company were small traders and poor loafers. At a fair, operettas reflecting the life of ordinary people were quite popular. Plays reflecting palace intrigues could also have great appeal if they were revised to suit audiences' taste.

In rural areas, performances were put up at marketplaces and country fairs. It is from marketplaces, temple fairs and old-style theaters that Peking Opera as a classical art gradually entered the life of city people.

A scene of *Love between the Living and Dead* (*ren gui qing*), a Peking Opera made into a movie. Photo by courtesy of China Film Archives.

Tanghui, or Performance at A Private Party

Tanghui, or performance at a private party, was an important form of performance in Beijing from the last years of the Ming Dynasty to 1949 when New China was founded. When a theatrical company was invited to put on shows at a private gathering outside a commercial theater, such as a private residence, a guildhall or a restaurant, that is called *tanghui*. A *tanghui* could also involve good performers of several theatrical companies who performed in the same shows.

A *tanghui* was held to celebrate a happy event such as a wedding and could last a whole day or at least half a day. Occasionally, theatrical companies jointly held benefit performances (for victims of natural disasters, for example). The list of plays and performers were all specially arranged; and the *tanghui* sponsor could select plays. Performers were selected from different theatrical companies in the city. As long as a *tanghui* sponsor had money, he could invite all famous performers in Beijing.

A *tanghui* had the following

94

A temple fair drawn by Sheng Xishan.

Theatrical program for Mei Lanfang's first performance in Shanghai in 1913. Photo by courtesy of Mei Lanfang Museum.

characteristics:

Firstly, the audience for a *tanghui* was not as mixed as that in a commercial theater; as a result, order and sanitary conditions at the venue of performance were much better than in a theater.

Secondly, a *tanghui* sponsor could organize the performance of plays that people of a prospective gathering liked most. Officials and citizens with power could even demand that performers abandon their acting assignment in a commercial theater to perform for their *tanghui*. Professional performers, out of fear or only too willing to flatter the powerful, did as told. Generally

Yang Chunxia, a famous *dan* player, stages a performance on a makeshift stage in Hebei. Photo taken in 1980.

speaking, therefore, the quality of performance at a *tanghui* was better than that in a commercial theater.

Thirdly, a *tanghui* sponsor could volunteer to participate in *tanghui* performances; and some fans requested that they play roles in the same show with famous professional performers. This often resulted in strange or even laughable performances.

Fourthly, at *tanghui* performances, audiences could eat and drink; women were allowed to watch performances (sometimes behind screens or on the second floor). At the time, this was not possible in commercial theaters.

Thanks to good material conditions, *tanghui* refined Peking Opera performance. In the first two decades of the 20th century, box office prices for famous actors who were frequent *tanghui* performers shot up. *Tanghui* made it possible for famous

In 1925, Mei Lanfang put on a tanghui, or performance at a private party. Photo by courtesy of Mei Lanfang Museum.

actors of different theatrical companies to act on the same stage. They discussed acting skills, learned from each other and competed for fame. This naturally led to a general improvement of their singing and acting skills.

Infatuated fans loved *tanghui*. These people would not miss a single performance by the actor they adored. A *tanghui* did not sell tickets, but they had a way of getting into a residence or guildhall, venue for a *tanghui* performance. Wearing clean clothes and carrying a gift package, they went through the gate when it was most crowded. Gatekeepers, taken in by their manners, usually let them in. Once inside, they would enjoy shows without fear of being bothered.

Amateur Performers

Peking Opera fans who double as amateur performers

are called *piaoyou*. *Piaoyou* reportedly appeared in the reign of Emperor Qianlong (1736-1795) of the Qing Dynasty. *Piaoyou* staged performances generally to a limited number of audiences and mainly for self-enjoyment. Many amateurs were better educated than professional performers and were interested in studying the art of Peking Opera, including plays, verses, singing styles, word phonetics and performing styles of different acting schools. Some well-known amateur performers can sing as well as do acrobatic fighting; some of them can even play a variety of roles, including *sheng* (male character), *chou* (clown) and *dan* (female character). Their attitude of striving for the perfect and their dedication to Peking Opera are absent in ordinary Peking Opera fans. *Piaoyou* as the core of Peking Opera audiences has played the role of raising audiences' overall level of appreciating Peking Opera and promoting the improvement of performing skills on the part of actors and actresses.

The place where amateur performers gather is called *piaofang*. A *piaofang* can be the home of a Peking Opera fan, or it can be a public place. By extension, it can also mean performance by amateurs. A complete *piaofang* must have the participation of three kinds of amateurs: those who sing, those who give musical accompaniment and those who watch.

A gathering of *piaoyou*, or amateur performers.

Amateur Peking Opera performers also gather regularly in parks in many Chinese cities, singing and acting largely for self-enjoyment. Their love of Peking Opera has enriched their life in their spare time.

In Beijing and Shanghai *piaofang* as a cultural activity has boomed in recent

Pi, everyday dress for woman.
photo by Yao Tianxin.

years. Amateur performers have set up loose organizations of their own and hold performing contests on the stage. A *piaofang* involving dozens of retired diplomats in Beijing puts up performances regularly and invites famous Peking Opera performers to give lectures. In the two cities, there are even *piaofangs* involving foreigners. The rebirth of *piaofang* is characteristic of our times. The getting together of Peking Opera lovers for self-amusement has become a fashionable leisure activity.

To become a Peking Opera *piaoyou*, one has to become a Peking Opera fan first. And before becoming a fan, one usually has accumulated many hours of watching Peking Opera performance and listening to Peking Opera singing. Some people are addicted to Peking Opera. The more they watch, the better they love Peking Opera to become out-and-out fans.

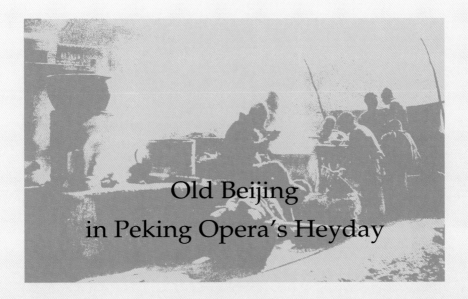

Old Beijing
in Peking Opera's Heyday

Peking Opera had its heyday in the 1930s when there were more than 10 theaters in Beijing alone, most of them scattered in the Qianmen area. This is a big number given the fact that Beijing at the time was quite small.

Residents of the area and traveling businessmen living in dingy hotels there were Peking Opera's principal audiences.

In the 1920s and 1930s, Peking Opera was a fashionable and important entertainment. Compared with other forms of entertainment, it held absolute dominance. Liu Zengfu is a Peking Opera specialist as well as a renowned physiologist. He recalls that when he attended Tsinghua University, the first thing he did when Sunday came was to get over his "opera addiction" by watching a Peking Opera at one of the theaters. Once his German teacher, a foreigner, cancelled the German lesson for the following Monday, saying he had to attend a friend's wedding on Sunday evening in the city. But when Liu sat in a theater for a Peking Opera performance on Sunday evening, he saw his German teacher sitting right in front of him. Teacher and student exchanged knowing smiles.

In early 1938 Yang Xiaolou, a master Peking Opera actor, died at the age of 61. Almost all famous Peking Opera performers attended his funeral. His fans and audiences all turned out to say good-bye to their beloved actor. The fact that an

Beijing in the 1910s and 1920s: the camel train was entering the city.

Food stalls in a Beijing street in the 1920s.

actor's death caused such a sensation in the city was quite unprecedented in the history of Peking Opera.

The birth and development of Peking Opera needed to have a proper environment. And old Beijing provided just such an environment. The Yanshou Temple Street south of present-day Hepingmen reflects the life of old Beijing. It is a largely deserted small street today. But in the 1930s and 1940s, the street, which was about 250 meters long, was flanked by more than 100 shops, of which seven sold condiments, six food grains, six breakfast, six pork, four mutton and four general merchandise. In addition, there were shops for noodles, cakes, dried and fresh fruits, soy sauce, sesame oil, bean curd, vermicelli, paper, tea, cloth, cotton and shoes as well as restaurants, teahouses, tailor shops, pharmacies, public baths, barber shops, galvanized iron shops and electrical materials shops. Workshops followed traditions in the trade they plied and the way of conducting transactions. Many people in opera circles lived near the Yanshou Temple Street since childhood.

National Opera Pictorial launched in 1932 carries treatises on Peking Opera and performers' articles. Photo by courtesy of Mei Lanfang Muserm

In 1927 Shuntian Times in Beijing held the first public poll for China's best *dan* players. This is a ticket distributed with the newspaper. Photo by courtesy of Mei Lanfang Museum.

The *paper-cuts* are images of Peking Opera characters.

Today, the street is still there. But gone are the shops and the ambience of business and cultural activities. Life scenes seen in the heyday of Peking Opera have disappeared from the surroundings of today's residents.

Brick carving with opera figures on the wall of an opera buiding.

Modern Peking Operas

From its very beginning, Peking Opera was closely connected with the culture of the national capital. Classic plays re-acting events of past dynasties constitute the bulk of Peking Opera repertoire. And Peking Opera performers improve their acting skills by playing roles in classic plays. So-called "modern plays" appeared as early as the early 20th century. These refer to operas telling stories that took place in the Qing and the Republic of China periods. Costume was also different from the traditional variety. Mei Lanfang at a young age came up with a number of new plays such as *Deng Xiagu* (*deng xia gu*, telling the story of Deng Xiagu helping her sister and sister-in-law escape persecution by their relatives) and *A Strand of Hemp* (*yi lu ma*, telling the life story of a talented girl and her simpleton husband). During the Second World War, a new play titled *Three Campaigns against the Zujiazhuang Village* (*san da zhu jia zhuang*), which is based on *The Water Margin*, was staged to

In the 1910s and 1920s, Mei Lanfang put on some modern-theme plays which revealed the oppression of Chinese women. Picture shows Mei in one of the plays. Photo by courtesy of Mei Lanfang Museum.

inspire people in their resistance against Japanese aggression. But there had been no large-scale performance of modern plays until the 1960s.

In the 1950s and 1960s, the practice of staging only classic plays among Peking Opera troupes faced grave challenges. Like other art forms, it was necessary for Peking Opera to let images of ordinary workers and peasants become leading roles on the theatrical stage. The idea that art and literature should serve politics became mainstream thought. In 1963, the Ministry of Culture required theatrical troupes to write and perform Peking Operas with a modern theme for national performance. In 1964, "National Performance of Modern Peking Operas before Fellow Artists for the Purpose of Discussion and Emulation" pushed to a climax activities of creating and staging modern-theme Peking Operas. A total of 37 plays were staged, and performance lasted 37 days and attracted 330,000 audiences. State leaders watched performances, too.

After the start of the Cultural Revolution (1966-1976), Jiang Qing, Mao Zedong's wife, led the art and literary circles in creating and staging five modern revolutionary Peking Operas – *Taking Tiger Mountain by Strategy* (*zhi qu wei hu shan*), *The Red Lantern* (*hong deng ji*), *Sha Jia Creek* (*sha jia bang*), *On the Docks* (*hai gang*) and *Raid on the White Tiger Regiment* (*qi xi bai hu tuan*). And together with two ballets and a symphony, they were called "Eight Revolutionary Model Plays." During the ten years, performance of all classic Peking Operas was banned. Radio stations broadcast and taught singing sections of these plays day in and day out (there were few television sets in the country then). Schools often organized performances of sections of the "model plays." Many people learned

The Red Lantern, a revolutionary model play. Photo taken in 1967

the plays by heart. The "model plays" became the standard for artistic creation in the country. They exerted influence over literature, painting, drama, traditional opera, dancing and music. Many accomplished artists were subjected to persecution during the Cultural Revolution; and some left the Peking Opera stage forever. Inheritance of traditional Peking Opera was forced to stop.

Revolutionary modern Peking Opera was quite different from the traditional one. Themes catered to political needs; movements of performers were closer to life; makeup was simplified; costume and stage settings were truer to reality; and Western musical instruments were introduced, with music aimed at stimulating a revolutionary fervor. It is not until 1978, two years after the end of the Cultural Revolution, that traditional Peking Opera made its difficult re-appearance on the stage.

Taking Tiger Mountain by Strategy, a revolutionary model play.
Photo taken in 1975.

The Chinese nowadays have mixed feelings about the "revolutionary model plays." Some people are strongly opposed to them because of their unhappy experiences in the Cultural Revolutions; others cannot forget them because these plays accompanied them in their adolescence; there are even people who, in a nostalgic fervor, performed them on the stage once again. There are also people who, while disapproving of the tendency of political interference in artistic creation as evidenced strongly in the "model plays," speak positively of their artistic accomplishment.

During the Cultural Revolution (1966-1976), actors and actresses of the Beijing Peking Opera Troupe staged performances and picked tea with farmers in Zhejiang.
Photo taken in 1975.

The town of Sha Jia Bang has become a tourist destination thanks to the revolutionary model play *Sha Jia Creek*, which has made it famous.

Close to 30 years have passed since the heyday of the "model plays." It is worthwhile to look at them from today's perspective. All these plays bear a distinct brand of a particular historical period, and extol a brand of heroism. Many well-known performers at the time played roles in these plays. Their level of acting was fairly high and their singing was pleasant to listen to. And singing is much more important than the plot. That is why these "revolutionary model plays" continue to have audiences today.

Attempts have continued to create modern plays. It is embarrassing to note, however, that, although quite a number of new plays have been created, none of them has surpassed the "model plays" in artistic attainment. In addition, because of less publicity than that for the "model plays" in their day, these new plays have had little impact.

Peking Opera has been passed down through oral instructions and face-to-face teachings. It developed into a system and came to maturity 60-70 years ago. For acting in Peking Opera, different schools have their respective unique "winning secrets," which in the past were not easily passed onto people outside their respective circles. On the history and traditions of Peking Opera, it is not advisable for later generations to take a simplistic attitude of judging what is correct and what is wrong. Watching a Peking Opera performance involves a spectator's own cultural interest and way of appreciating the beautiful. Only with a penetrating spirit can one gain the ability to really appreciate the charms of Peking Opera. And Peking Opera is a "slow" art. For internal innovation of Peking Opera as well as for enjoyment of the art form, a "gradual approach," rather than "abrupt change," is favored. This is because such an approach better reflects the soul of Peking Opera.

Singing, Dancing and Acting Skills

In the beginning, a Chinese theatrical performance consisted mainly of singing and dancing. Singing, dancing and acting skills constitute a Peking Opera performer's basic accomplishments.

In some Peking Opera plays, one aspect is emphasized rather than a combination of the three. As a result, we have singing shows, recitation shows and plot shows. A typical singing show is *Visiting the palace Twice* (*er jin gong*), in which not only are emotions expressed through singing but singing is used to indicate how characters walk. A typical dancing show is *The Cowherd and the Village Lass* (*xiao fang niu*), in which a cowherd and a village girl dance a lot without much singing. In plot shows, singing, dancing and other skills are largely discarded; they win audiences with intriguing stories. Such shows include *Catching the County Magistrate in a Dough Vat* (*da mian gang*), *Beating the Town God* (da cheng huang) and *A Maid's Choice of the Husband's Family* (san bu yuan yi), in which a clown or a beautiful woman is usually the leading character.

There are also operas with a grand combination of singing, dancing and acting skills. These include *The Battle of Wits* (*qun ying hui*), *Borrowing the East Wind* (*jie dong feng*), *the Huarong Pass* (*hua rong dao*) and *Ganlu Monastery* (*gan lu si*), which involve a full range of roles and all ways of portrayal.

Zhang Xuejin (second from left), a pupil of the Ma Lianliang Performing School, plays a role in a *lao sheng* opera. Photo by Wang Kexin.

Operas of different styles have different audiences. Singing, recitation and plot shows are for connoisseurs, who know where the beauty of such plays lies; whereas comprehensive shows are for the laymen, who love fun and excitement.

"Music is made out of every sound, and dancing out of every movement." This is a feature of Peking Opera.

"Sound" in Peking Opera refers first of all to a performer's singing and recitation. It also includes the sounds of nature and animals – the sounds of wind, rain and thunder, a dog's bark, the mewing of a cat, etc. By "music is made out of every

Substituting acrobatic fighting with dancing. Photo by Wu Gang.

The hat is used to express different feelings in Peking Opera. Picture shows a *Xiao sheng* throwing away his official hat at hearing news of his parents' death. Photo taken in 1961.

sound" is meant that once such sounds come from the stage, they must all sound pleasant to the ear, no matter how they actually do.

Singing is of the first importance in Peking Opera. Most people go to a Peking Opera theater to hear singing. Through singing, characters engage in dialogues and speak to themselves. In Peking Opera, actors and actresses sing according to different tunes and rhythms. For different plays and different sections of singing in one play, there is much room to select tunes.

What are acting skills, or *xigong* in Peking Opera? These refer to skills that conform with acting conventions in Peking Opera. Traditionally, they refer to skill-related rules and methods that have been passed down relating to acting with the hand, eyes, the body, the hair and steps. Such rules are reflected in singing, recitation, acting and acrobatics. Singing should have modulation in tone, be sweet and complicated; body movements should be agreeable to look at, with each step and

Acrobatic fighting in Peking Opera. Photo by Wu Gang.

Dancing that portrays going to a tryst. Photo by Zhang Zhaoji.

hand movement complying with required rules and forms. Every role requires a set of basic skills. Learners cannot master them unless they practice them year after year with great dedication.

There are also some skills that are called *juehuo*, meaning feats or stunts. In Peking Opera, there was once a skill called *qiaogong* that portrays steps made by a woman with bound feet. At the time, all Peking Opera performers were men with big feet. Someone invented the method of having a male actor's feet supported by wooden sticks to perform such steps. An actor needed to practice two to three years to master the technique. Besides, fans are frequently used in Peking Opera. In *hongniang the Maidservant (hong niang)*, the maid uses a round fan to catch

Women Generals of the Yang Family, a traditional Peking Opera.

butterflies. In other plays, ladies usually use folding fans. As performances involving fans grew in number, there came into being a so-called fan skill, which has become a basic acting skill in Peking Opera. Fans are used for different purposes: for cooling, or for helping convey a meaning, such as emphasizing what the user is saying or indicating a distance. In Peking Opera, there are also handkerchief skill, beard skill, hair-throwing skill and chair skill.

"Realms" of Acting

Peking Opera performers devide performance into three realms : "being accurate," "being beautiful" and "having a lingering charm."

What is "being accurate?" To learn acting in Peking Opera, a kid needs to learn basic skills first of all. He needs to practice every minute movement over and over again. He begins by imitating until his movements, postures, eye expression, singing style, pronunciation, intonation, etc. are judged to meet required standards, or required accuracy. For a performer, rehearsal and actual performance consist in a combination of conventionalized movements.

Young actors can participate in performances if their acting meets standards required of each role category. In the West, individuality is emphasized in acting. An actor who does not have "individuality" is not regarded as a good one. Not so in Peking Opera. An actor goes through two stages before becoming fully qualified. In the first stage, he needs to master singing and acting skills required in a particular play. In the second stage, with the actor's artistic accomplishment and pursuit permeating into the roles he plays, his acting may assume some "individuality," which is not lost on mature audiences. This is the second stage of acting.

What is "being beautiful?" This refers to a performer, armed with a fine artistic perception, being able to portray the personalities of characters accurately. "Being beautiful" is a sublimation of accuracy, a shift from emphasis on acting skills to

112

Gai Jiaotian practiced martial skill in the courtyard of his residence.

Yuan Shihai, a well-known *jing* role player, practiced martial skill.

Eye expression is most important in Peking Opera. As captured on film, Mei Lanfang had 48 eye expressions. Photo by courtesy of Mei Lanfang Museum.

emphasis on aesthetic values. This requires a performer to have fine artistic skills and creativity.

The third realm is that acting should have a "lingering charm." What is charm, which is invisible? But frequent theatergoers feel it. It might be said that charm is a tacit understanding between a veteran performer and his audiences, the appreciation and comprehension of unique Peking Opera acting, the ultimate beauty of Peking Opera, which reflects the common spirit of chinese culture. Fans have standards for "lingering charm." Cheng Yanqiu's singing is generally regarded as having such a charm. It is described as "being gentle as weeping and lingering as a thread." Audiences savor its aftertaste long after they have left the theater. This also applies to recitation, postures, dance movements and acrobatic fighting.

Performers sometimes play roles outside their usual line. This requires great artistic attainment and a wide scope of performing skills on the part of the performer. In the photo, Cheng Yanqiu plays the usual *dan* role, whereas Shang Xiaoyun, also a *dan* role impersonator, plays a *xiao sheng*.

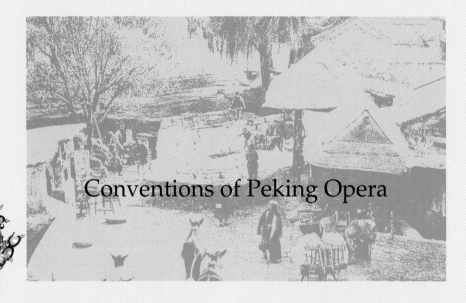

Conventions of Peking Opera

In Peking Opera acting, attention is paid to both symbolism and the conversion of movements into graceful dancing. Imitation brings out symbolism. A performer imitates and beautifies life's actions. For example, he opens and closes a door where there is no door at all. This is true of mounting or dismounting a horse, going upstairs or coming downstairs, going on board a ship or leaving a ship. At the same time, movements on the Peking Opera stage should be dance-like, have a rhythm and are pleasant to look at. This necessitates exaggeration and pantomimic variations. A combination of symbolism and movement-to-graceful-dancing conversion has resulted in conventionalized acting that is unique to Peking Opera. That is to say, many human actions have gradually been adapted for the theatrical stage and fallen into fixed patterns to become intricate conventions which generations of performers have conformed with and which people are familiar with.

Conventionalized acting in Peking Opera does not come into existence overnight. It is accumulated by a succession of performers and passed down from generation to generation. While standards are to be followed, a break with accepted routine is allowed. Acting conventions develop in the process of being inherited.

In a theatrical company, performers abide by the rule of "wearing ragged clothes rather than the wrong costume." A performer certainly knows what costume to

wear when he plays a certain role in a play. Wearing
wrong costume does not accord with the plot, nor is it
acceptable to the audience. Costuming conventions are
a spin-off of acting stylization; and, in turn, it reinforces
acting stylization in Peking Opera. As most Peking
Operas tell historical stories, the forms of costume are
fixed and categorized. Generally, theatrical costume
is divided into five categories: *mang* (the ceremonial
robe embroidered with patterns of four-toed dragon
and sea-waves worn by emperors or high-ranking
officials), *kao* (the warriors' suit of armor), *zhe* (the
lined coat), *pi* (mantle worn by male or female) and *yi*
(other costumes). Whoever wears a yellow robe with
python patterns is an emperor; and whoever wears a
blue gown and a black hat a scholar. A character's
identity is easily known by what he wears.

Peking Opera costume took shape during the Qing
Dynasty but was based on clothes people wore during
the Ming Dynasty. The Palace Museum in Beijing
keeps a book titled An Outline of Wear, which lists the
costume of characters in close to 1,000 Peking Operas.

Facial makeup in Peking Opera aims to exaggerate
characters' facial color and features according to
requirements of portrayal. Face coloring for
the *sheng* role, the delineation of
eyebrows, the eye sockets and the
mouth for the *dan* role, and face
painting for the *jing* and *chou*
roles all have such an effect.

The most characteristic are *tie pian zi* for the *dan*
role and face painting for the *jing* and *chou* roles. By

The red-faced man on the left is Guan Yu, a general of the Three Kingdoms period. He does not wear his trademark *kao,* or a warrior's suit of armor. This shows that costume in Peking Opera is subordinate to perform requirements. Photo taken by Zhang Zhaoji.

tie pian zi is meant that long hair is painted on each side of a *dan*-role player's face and flower patterns are pasted above his brows. The greatest benefit of this is to change the look of the player's natural face. In the case of a male actor playing a *dan* role, this makes the face more feminine. Using colors to create facial images is a tradition in the history of the Chinese theater. This applies mostly to *jing* (painted face) and *chou* (clown) role types.

In the long process of development, every character in each opera has acquired a unique makeup image, and such makeup conventions have won recognition from the audience. As soon as a character comes onto

the stage, the audience, on the basis of the character's facial makeup and costume, would immediately know whether the character is a kind-hearted, evil, loyal, treacherous, good-looking or ugly person. And this has an impact on the stage effect of a play in question.

The *dan* players on the right wears a soft *kao* (a warrior's suit of armor without flags) The costume of the two characters is slightly different from the usual style of today.

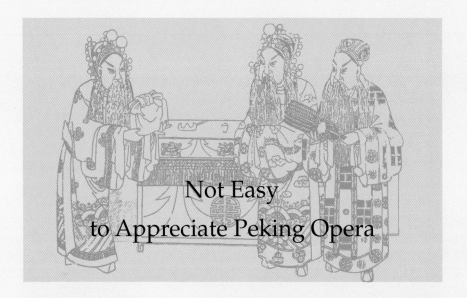

Not Easy
to Appreciate Peking Opera

People often say that, to be able to enjoy music, one has to have musical ears and that to enjoy an opera, one has to have opera eyes. This is true of Peking Opera, too.

Liu Haisu, a Peking Opera fan as well as a traditional Chinese painting artist, once wrote an article, in which he likens the acting styles of different performing schools of Peking Opera to traditional paintings of different styles. He says: Mei Lanfang's performing style is like a finely drawn, bright-colored peony with leaves brought out in subtle black lines; Tan Xinpei's style is like an ink and wash painting where brilliance is hidden in plainness; and Zhou Xinfang's style resembles a great pine tree with strong, upright branches brought out in black ink. What he means is that there are similarities between different classic Chinese arts.

From the late 18th century, *kunqu* opera originating in south China began declining. Purists had kept improving its conventions and singing style, leaving it burdened with increasing limitations. Audiences who got tired of *kunqu* opera complained that it was too long, too slow, too perfect, too refined and too rigid. This reflected a popular orientation in the appreciation of classic art at a time of change.

Peking Opera, on the other hand, has become a symbol of the traditional Chinese theater in modern times. It represents a unique artistic integration at a time when modern civilization is superseded by contemporary civilization in China. In Peking Opera, folk spirit is combined with palace interest; and southern China customs come together with northern China lifestyles. In its ascension, Peking Opera, transcending classes and geographical division, demonstrated great vitality. Peking Opera's aesthetic qualities – combinations of form and spirit, of abstractness and substance and of sound and pantomime, and its time and spatial freedoms – are all connected with this integration. For a long historical period, China's theatrical culture including Peking Opera created beauty as well as entertainingness.

In acting style, Peking Opera has evolved from simplicity and plainness to refinement and elegance and affected the development of other types of the traditional Chinese theater. Peking Opera has enriched and perfected the performing art of the traditional Chinese theater. But, despite having a rich repertoire, Peking Opera has failed to leave behind

119

Much acting in Peking Opera is borrowed from *kunqu* opera. Using body movements and finger skills, Mei Lanfang depicts a lady in five states. Photo by courtesy of Mei Lanfang Museum.

outstanding works. This indicates a major turning point in the history of Chinese classic theater: theatrical activities centering on the creation of theatrical plays gave way to theatrical activities centering on performance. The benefit of this consists in a full development of the performing art – the natural core of the theatrical art. And it is here that the beauty of China's theatrical art lies.

When a Western-style opera or concert is in progress, no sound from the audience is usually allowed, not even applause. Late audiences are not led to their seats until an act is over. Peking Opera is different. Audiences may shout "Bravo" when acting is at its best. When Cheng Changgeng, founder of Peking Opera, performed in the imperial palace, the emperor could not help shouting his appreciation. People have unique ways of enjoying Peking Opera. Some take a particular liking for its singing, others love to watch acting by particular performers. Audiences well versed in Peking Opera know when to shout "Bravo" and when not to.

Some fans would say: "Peking Opera is quite complicated. The subject of costume alone can take a lifetime to study." Indeed, Peking Opera is Greek to those Chinese who rarely go to a theater, let alone to foreigners. When an actor wears wrong costume, they would not notice the error; nor would they find it when an actress's singing gets out of tune. Watching an opera becomes watching excitement. Plays with a lot of acrobatic fighting are easier to understand. Audiences enjoy watching the fluttering costume of actors

Two teenagers put on a *wu sheng* play. Photo taken in 1956.

Han Shichang (right), a well-known *kunqu* opera actor, and Mei Lanfang put on a *kunqu* opera in 1957.

engaged in fierce fighting and listening to the slow or quick tempo sounds of clappers that denote deep night, thinking hard or perspiring with cold sweat upon suddenly waking up to a situation.

Then, why don't many young people like to watch Peking Opera today? One reason is the environment. If a person is surrounded by people who are Peking Opera fans, he may come to like Peking Opera, too, under their influence; and the opposite is true, too. Another reason may have to do with people's "places of origin." Dialects in China are numerous and differ widely. People born in southern China are not familiar

with pronunciation in Beijing and cannot easily see the beauty of Peking Opera.

But there are people who easily come to like Peking Opera. Ione Meyer, who was born in Scotland and now lives in London, is head of the UK Peking Opera Society. In Paris in 1989, she watched a Peking Opera performance for the first time and immediately loved it. She later explained that stylized movements, beautiful costume, high-pitched singing and extraordinary style of Peking Opera gave her great inspiration and encouragement. She had an idea: to go to Beijing to learn Peking Opera. At the end of 1989, with help from her friends, she came to the Beijing Opera School which trains adolescent pupils. The school was moved by her love of Peking Opera, accepted her as a Peking Opera student. From September 1991, at the age of 27, she became the second foreign student in the school. After three years of hard learning and practice, Ione Meyer learned to play roles in *Hu Jia Zhuang Village* (*hu jia zhuang*), *Exchange of Blows in a Restaurant* (*da dian*), *The Battle of Jinshan* (*zhan jin shan*), *The Maid in Heaven Showering Flowers* (*tian nu san hua*), *Farewell My Concubine* (*ba wang bie ji*) and other classic operas. And she has learned to speak fluent Chinese. After her return to Britain, Ione Meyer was determined to introduce Peking Opera to the West. In 1994, she founded the UK Peking Opera Society, whose members are young teachers and students of London's institutions of higher learning who love oriental art. She invited Jiang Aibing, a former actor of the Shanghai Peking Opera Troupe having emigrated to London, to serve as their teacher. Members of the society often stage Peking Opera shows on campuses. They also participated in the recent Edinburgh Art Festival.

In recent years, more foreigners have come to China to learn Peking Opera at opera schools like Ione Meyer. After several years of study, their performance reaches a level that surprises their Chinese colleagues and audiences.

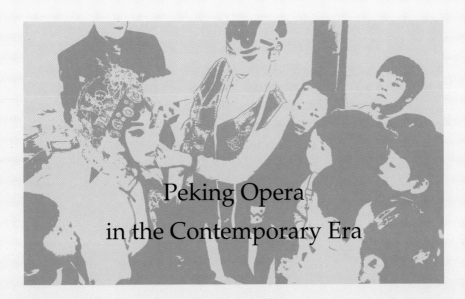

Peking Opera
in the Contemporary Era

After the founding of the People's Republic of China, the government appropriated a special fund for the development of Peking Opera. Much progress was made in Peking Opera's performance, personnel training, play writing, music composition, education, research, legacy preservation, publishing and external exchanges. Performers entered state-owned or collective opera companies and became employees of the state. Nationwide, the number of Peking Opera troupes above the county level reached 100, and opera schools across the country trained Peking Opera professionals.

In the 1949-1964 period, a succession of outstanding performers brightened the Peking Opera stage. The four great *dan* role performers put on new plays. Their successors who came to maturity in the 1930s and 1940s became the mainstay of the stage. At the same time, a new crop of performers trained by New China were beginning to claim their place of prominence and took part in the creation of modern Peking Operas. These performers include Li Shaochun, Du Jinfang, Yuan Shihai, Gao Yuqian, Zhao Yanxia, Liu Changyu, Zhou Hetong, Tan Yuanshou, Ma Changli, Zhang Xuejin, Li Chongshan, Guan Sushuang, Li Rongwei, Fang Rongxiang, Song Yuqing and Tong Zhiling.

In the meantime, external exchanges increased. The China Peking Opera Troupe,

and opera troupes in Beijing, Shanghai and other cities kept putting up performances in foreign countries, winning acclaim wherever they went.

With the development of technologies, people can now watch Peking Opera performances not only in theaters but also in the cinema and on the TV screen. They can also hear Peking Opera singing over the radio and by playing the audio tape and CD. On holidays, Peking Opera performers offer programs at evening parties that are broadcast live by TV and radio stations. When it goes from the stage to the screen, Peking Opera has shed some of its performing conventions. At the same time, people's interest has changed. They prefer performances that are entertaining, popular, pluralistic and in vogue. This has doubtlessly exerted a big impact on Peking Opera as a traditional stage art.

In the last 20-30 years, the Peking Opera market has shrunk, making it difficult for some performing troupes to survive. Some performers have been forced to take roles in films and TV plays, or become pop singers, TV hostesses or even fashion models. Some members of Peking Opera orchestras have joined pop music groups. In its competition with popular commercial culture, Peking Opera is fighting a losing battle. The number of people who love to watch Peking Opera has been declining. Younger generations have a strong sense of estrangement for traditional Peking Operas that reflect ancient life. "I don't understand Peking Opera and I don't like to watch it" is a common attitude among young people.

Peking Opera is part of a traditional culture. It is unavoidable for people of the present age to feel estranged from it. The Chinese government has paid great attention to the promotion, protection and inheritance of traditional culture. Leaders of the country have often attended Peking Opera parties. Peking Opera has been playing an important role in international cultural exchanges, with numerous troupes staging performances abroad. Great attention has been paid to opera education. Television stations have held national Peking Opera performing contests that are broadcast live. China Central Television Station has opened a channel (CCTV-11) that is dedicated exclusively to broadcasting Chinese traditional operas, including Peking Opera. The station also offers lectures on the basics of Peking Opera and makes Peking Opera films and TV plays. For several consecutive years, the station has

sponsored national performing contests by Peking Opera *piaoyou*, or amateur performers. In recent years, the China Peking Opera Festival has been held three times, and the occasions were great holidays for fans and Peking Opera circles. The government has also spent a huge amount of money creating images for prerecorded Peking Opera singing by a great number of masters, most of whom have passed away. People involved worked eight years to complete the rescue project. Many famous actors and actress of the present age, in providing images for past masters, have had the opportunity to train and show themselves. Thanks to the successful execution of the project, more than 300 plays now have images as well as the sound of

The Nanjing Peking Opera Troupe holds an open house for children. Picture kept by photocome.com

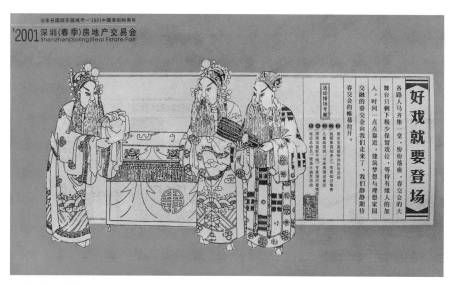

An advertisement for a real estate trade fair carried by Shenzhen Special Economic Zone Daily of April 12, 2001. The advertisement features a scene of *Offering Chengdu*, a traditional Peking Opera, to attract attention. Picture kept by Wang Shucun.

singing. Resulting works of the project can not only serve as valuable teaching materials for Peking Opera students but also meet the need of fans and audiences to enjoy masterpieces. Works of the project provide young audiences of today with a convenient medium to know today's crop of outstanding performers and hear the charming singing of past masters.

In 1982, amid active exchanges between Chinese and Western cultures, Qi Xiaoyun (1930-2003), an actress good at playing the painted face role, sang arias in English in a Peking Opera "Othello." She also used English to sing songs in traditional operas *Judge Bao and his Sister-in-law* and *Case of the Ungrateful Husband's Execution* and translated and adapted *the Baccae*, a Greek tragedy by Euripides, into a Peking Opera.

In May of 2002, at the centennial of Nanjing

University, a group of foreigners clad in ancient Chinese theatrical costume performed in English the traditional Peking Opera *Judge Bao and the Case of Qin Xianglian*. They won repeated applause from the audience with their singing, recitation, acting and fighting that have a genuine Peking Opera flavor. Professor Elizabeth Wichmann-Walczak, chairwoman of Theater and Dance Department of University of Hawaii, translated the play and served as director. All actors and actresses staging the show are students of the university majoring in music and the theater. In 1979, Elizabeth Wichmann-Walczak enrolled in Nanjing University as a student of the Chinese language and Chinese theater. She learned Peking Opera from Shen Xiaomei, a Peking Opera performer of the Mei Lanfang School. After returning to the United States, she was determined to put up Peking Opera in English. After half a year's hard work, English-language Peking Opera *Judge Bao and the Case of Qin Xianglian* was staged in February, 2002 for the public in Hawaii. A total of ten performances were staged, all to a full house.

Against today's open and plural cultural background, Peking Opera as a traditional art of the Chinese nation is understood and liked by an increasing number of foreigners. This is closely connected with the participation

A *dan* role in *Drunken Beauty* performed by a contemporary performer. Photo by Zhao Dechun.

Atlanta uses Peking Opera to promote the Olympics it hosts in 1996.

of Mei Lanfang, Cheng Yanqiu and other artists of the old generation in Chinese-foreign cultural exchanges and comparative studies of Chinese and Western theaters when Peking Opera was in its heyday. In the last century, footsteps of Peking Opera troupes have covered 40 countries and regions in the world. They have made important contributions to publicizing traditional Chinese culture, promoting international cultural exchanges and enhancing understanding and friendship between the Chinese people and peoples of the rest of the world.

An American student plays the lead role in *Drunken Beauty*, a traditional Peking Opera, at an evening party in Nanjing University.